Standing Fast
was published in the United States by
JTC Sports, Inc.
PO Box 513
Apex, NC 27502
(919) 303-6611
Fax (919) 303-7111

Publisher: Janice T. Cheves
Design by: AGA Graphics
Cover Design: Collins Integrated Resources
Cover Photos by: J. Brett Whitesell
Back Cover Photos by: Allsport and J. Brett Whitesell
Additional Photos: Phil Stephens, J. Brett Whitesell, Mary Harvey, Mike Stahlschmidt, Jon Van Woerden, Kristine Lilly, Doug Menuez, Allsport, Colleen Hacker, Eva Ferara.

Editorial assistance provided by: Jan Cheves, Carter Cheves, Doug Herakovich, Eva Ferara, Harry Nash, Lorraine Nash, Mick Hoban.

First Printing June 1997

ISBN 1-887791-04-3

Printed in the United States of America

I dedicate this book

to all those who are called to

STAND FAST

in the pursuit of their dreams.

Michelle and her father during a post-Olympic climb

About the Title

I WAS SITTING ATOP A HUGE ROCK FORMATION THAT afforded me the view of a few frozen lakes, flowing rivers and the snow-covered mountain ranges both nearby and on the horizon. Below me was the valley where we had pitched camp.

The wind was biting cold, but I had stuffed myself in the shelter of an overhang that allowed me to feel the warmth from the sun overhead. It was a great day, one of those days that is indelibly marked in your memory. I could have sat there forever. For me, it was a few days respite from the spotlight and the demands of being a public figure and gold medalist. Don't get me wrong, I love the public and our faithful fans, but there are times when I need to be alone, times when I need to feel insignificant. The mountains do that for me. The mountains make everything so incredibly simple and allow me the chance to remember that my place in this world is fleeting and small at best.

I pulled my book from my pack and began reading. Every couple paragraphs I would glance away from the page to take in the majestic surroundings and let the meaning of the words sink in. The book is a study about three letters (in the Bible) sent to the Philippians, Colossians, and Thessalonians. Paul, a disciple/follower of Christ many years ago, wrote them to encourage this group of disheartened Christians. I love Paul. He is intense, committed, strong of character, and encouraging to those around him. A phrase he wrote and the interpretation that followed struck me hard. In one passage (Phil 4:1) Paul is talking to the Philippians (an early church of Christ), who are struggling and battling for their faith, and he says, "Stand fast in the Lord." A study done by William Barclay, another cool and very intense guy, goes on to explain specifically what "Stand fast in the Lord" means. I quote: "The word Paul uses for stand fast (skekete) is the word which would be used for a soldier standing fast in the shock of battle with the enemy surging down upon him."

That hit home. I felt like a warrior. I could so clearly see myself standing defiant in the middle of a battlefield fighting and battling the "enemy" that surged around me. So many times, I had stood firm and fought them off one by one in my quest to become the person I wanted to be or to go after the dream I had wanted so much.

Whether you are a bible believer or not, and whether you take these words to have spiritual meaning or not, isn't so much the point. The thing that hit me was I have spent my entire life "standing fast." Not necessarily for God, but for my dreams, my ideals, and my character. I was this warrior amidst the crush of battle trying desperately to stand up to injury, illness, corruption, prejudice, discrimination, fear and uncertainty — stuff we fight all the time, day-in and day-out.

Only recently have I learned or tasted what Paul meant when he said "Stand fast in the Lord." The key words are "In the Lord." I had fought so many battles, but never *in the Lord.* Always in my own strength. The explanation Barclay gave was that as a Christian, the only way to do battle and be victorious was if we fought in God's strength and in His power and justification. When we step out on our own, we are walking directly into disaster and loss. I can testify to that. It has happened to me. Only in God's power can we endure and then finally, triumph. But here is the exciting, and even humbling, part: this battle is even more challenging and rewarding than the battles I had so willingly fought before. The battle I am now fighting is for life.

As you read my story, you will hopefully come to understand the many shades of meaning the title, "Standing Fast" represents. It is meant to describe my life, especially the last five or six years. But, just as Paul wrote to his crew, it is also meant as an encouragement ... maybe even a challenge.

(For more information on my faith and how you can further develop your own relationship with God, please see Appendix E in the back of this book.)

Thank You's and Acknowledgments

THERE ARE LOADS OF FOLKS TO THANK. ALL OF THESE people have been a huge part of my story and deserve more than a quick mention in the acknowledgments. But limited time and space will not allow me to give the full appreciation I hold for each of them. I love you, but this will have to do. Special thanks to the following:

To Tim Nash: Congratulations. You did what you set out to do — change peoples lives with your words. To Steve: Thanks for lending me the book (by William Barclay). It got thrashed during the hike, but I will buy you a new one ... Not! To my family: What else can I say? I love you. To my good and sometimes, insane friends, Goz, Hades, Eva, SallyMally, Barnface, The 3 Judys (and Steve), and The Buzzberg-Hallbergs: You studs. Thanks for believing in me. To Campus Crusade for Christ and Northland Community Church: You studs. Thank you for the prayers, support, and inspiration. To my Team: Go USA. You guys are the greatest. To my doctors, PT's (Rodney the Great), and trainers: Thanks — I.O.U. big time. To Reebok, who supported this venture all along: Thanks. To the CFIDS Association of America: Keep up Mission Impossible. We will win the battle one day soon. To my fans and the faithful supporters of women's soccer: We couldn't have done it without you. And lastly, thanks to Jesus Christ, the One who does it all for me every single day.

Thanks to you all. And to those of you who know you should be thanked, but I have completely forgotten (surprise) ... thank you, too.

With all my love,

Michelle

Introduction

ONCE A PROFESSOR IN A COLLEGE WRITING CLASS SPOUTED out a seemingly simple phrase. It was either one of his better moments, or one of the few comments to which I actually paid attention. Nonetheless, it stuck with me. "Truth," he said, "is stranger than fiction." He went on to explain that a true story, if told right, will always have more of an impact and be more memorable than anything a writer could possibly invent.

I now understand exactly what he meant. The story of Michelle Akers could not possibly be invented by a fiction writer. It is, at times, mind-boggling and parts of it cannot be explained through conventional wisdom. I consider myself extremely fortunate to have learned Michelle's whole story in a very convincing way — with the drama and emotion of the Olympic Games as a backdrop.

I first approached Michelle about this project in April of 1995 at a reception for the U.S. National Team in Charlotte, N.C. I asked her if she wanted to write a book, and she said, "Sure." That was about the extent of the conversation. I thought it would be a book about how she rose to the top of the women's soccer world — a nice little story about her training habits, her commitment to the sport, and it would be full of advice and tips for young players. No supreme truths, no fiction ... just a story about a soccer player. We didn't really talk about the book much until I met with her at the national team's training camp in Orlando a year later. We traded ideas, and she agreed to send her personal journals to get me started. I received her journals shortly before the Olympics and took them with me as I traveled to Orlando, Miami and Athens to watch the Olympics. I read through them as I watched her team march to the gold medal, and what I discovered was not at all what I expected.

I had known she was sick, but I didn't know the extent of her illness and suffering. Very few did. Her struggles with CFIDS were, however, spelled out very clearly in her journals. I had watched her get injured in the 1995 Women's World Cup, but never understood the impact that crushing disappointment had on her life. I knew she was a Christian, but didn't know why.

During my own odyssey through the Olympics, I read her journals on planes, in airports, in hotel rooms, in press boxes. Whenever I had some free time, I would read. Then I would go to Olympic matches and watch. I was one of the few in attendance who understood the courage and faith those games required of Michelle. Little by little, I began to understand the depth of her faith in God. I tried to find other explanations for her courage. I desperately wanted to discover some rational, concrete reason for her ability to persevere. But with each game and with each page of her journals, I came closer to the unmistakable conclusion that there was a greater force involved. Truth, it seemed, was indeed more powerful than fiction.

Before the 1996 Olympics, the only thing I had done religiously was avoid church. But I began attending St. Mark's Reformed Church in Burlington, N.C., regularly with my wife, Cheri, and five-year-old daughter, Allison. I found it enlightening and challenging. I learned that God has a plan for everyone, and I was glad to discover that you don't have to be struck by lightning to discover that plan. You can be a regular guy, like me.

I went to the Olympics uncertain of my future. The rigors of running a small publishing company were taking their toll on me and my partner. I knew changes had to be made, and I was struggling to figure out what they were. Then as I was re-reading Michelle's journals one day, I noticed how many times she mentioned the path on which God had put her. Then it dawned on me — her path included me. Well, it had never occurred to me that God had a plan for me. At about this same time, I heard a guy on TV say, "If you really want to make God laugh, tell him *your* plan." I decided to stop making plans, stop trying to orchestrate my life and stop trying to organize the people in it. I asked God to put me on his "To Do" list. He did, and my life has changed. Today, I can call myself a Christian.

There are many people to thank for their assistance in this project. First, I have to thank the people, whoever they are, who invented email. How do you do hundreds of interviews with someone suffering from a chronic illness? By email, and that's how every single interview for this book was done. I would send a load of questions off to Michelle, and when she was feeling up to it, she would answer them. It enabled her to go into more detail than she would have in a conventional interview, and it allowed her time to explain her thoughts to the fullest.

I also would like to thank my business partner Jan Cheves and her husband Carter for their support, input and direction. Cheri and Allison should be awarded medals for their patience with my late nights. Cheri also provided some key questions for Michelle in a formerly weak section of the book, and Allison's help checking emails was crucial. My parents, Harry and Lorraine Nash, and brother, Marty, provided input and constant support, and they have been great examples for me. Eva Ferara was crucial to the direction and focus of the book, as well as being a great source of background information and a good friend. Anson Dorrance, who enabled me to get into the book-writing business, gets a heart-felt thank you, and I would also like to thank Reverend Bob Disher of St. Mark's Church in Burlington for helping me with my overall direction and purpose. The people at Reebok provided resources and support to this project all along. And thanks to Laurie Gregg for sending me the Olympic highlight video, which was critical for details and accuracy. A special thanks needs to go out to all of Michelle's teammates, coaches and friends (yes, even Foudy and Gozley) for painting a picture of the true Michelle. I would also like to thank Michelle for letting me into her private life and for allowing me to join her on this enlightening journey. And thanks, I guess, for the nickname. In the future, you really don't have to identify yourself as Michelle Akers on a voice mail message after you say, "Hey, Nasher Face Tim-Dog!" Believe me, I know it's you. Lastly, I would like to thank God for showing me that I matter and for putting me on such an exciting and revealing path.

Tim Nash

Foreword

HALLEY'S COMET ONLY VISITS ONCE EVERY SEVENTY-FIVE years, more than the usual lifetime for humans. When it comes, people stay up all night and forego various duties just to catch a glimpse of this wonder. It's just what we humans do when something extraordinary enters our world. Michelle Akers is a wonder. Indeed, she is a wonder of wonders.

But unlike the comet, her mercurial career — her incredible battle against odds both internal and external — has been captured in this book. We get more than a passing glimpse. We get to catch the comet and hold it for in-depth examination.

I remember vividly, the first time I saw her. She was a typical spindly legged, somewhat impish, nine-year-old. But that's where any comparison to a typical nine-year-old girl ends. The first time I saw her, she was playing soccer, and she took to the task with a vengeance ... make that a fury. She hated anything that smacked of mediocrity. She despised losing (Vince Lombardi would have started her at middle linebacker). I thought she might become the first woman to play on my men's university team.

Since that day, she has gone on to become one of the great women of the world. She not only led her team to the first world championship in women's soccer, she has become a spokeswoman for the cause of women in general, as well as in soccer. And her journey continues.

Michelle's story is more than a journey. It's a pilgrimage, a modern day Pilgrim's Progress that has led her out of the darkness and into the light — God's light. However, the central focus of this story is not Christian, the warrior. The central character is a woman. It's a woman playing a sport that has long been held in the male bastions of the world. And this woman is playing it better than most of her male counterparts. And achieving excellence, achieving equality.

In his classic book, "Excellence", John W. Gardner wrote that his book was not only about excellence but more specifically about the conditions under which it was possible in our society. Moreover, he warned that any discussion of the topic must "inevitably include equality, the kind that can and must be honored and the kind that cannot be forced."

Michelle Akers is a walking compendium of excellence and equality. She has bucked all the tidal fronts of opposition from within — nagging injuries, the lingering, energy-sapping Chronic Fatigue Immune Dysfunction Syndrome. And she has battled outside forces — prejudice, put-downs and the preternatural resistance of those in her beloved sport of soccer. Through it all, she has more than survived. She has overcome. She has become a champion. John Gardner would be proud.

This is a book about a woman, about excellence, about beauty and about overcoming. And all who travel with Michelle through these pages, will be pleased, challenged, enlightened and guided in their own life's journey.

C. Cliff McCrath
Seattle Pacific University

Preface

CHRONIC FATIGUE IMMUNE DYSFUNCTION SYNDROME (CFIDS) is a serious and complex illness that affects many different body systems. The illness strikes men, women and children of all ages, ethnic backgrounds and socio-economic groups. The most common targets, however, are women between the ages of twenty-five and forty-five. There is no known cause and no known cure. Only in the past decade has the medical community made advancements in the study and understanding of CFIDS. The illness often goes unrecognized and is frequently misdiagnosed as Mononucleosis, Multiple Sclerosis, Fibromyalgia, Lyme Disease, Post-Polio Syndrome and auto-immune diseases such as Lupus.

Due to the medical community's inability to agree on the causes and symptoms, Chronic Fatigue Immune Dysfunction Syndrome is often referred to as Epstein-Barr Virus (EBV), Chronic Epstein-Barr Virus (CEBV), Chronic Fatigue Syndrome (CFS), Fibromyalgia (FM) and Myalgic Encephalomyelitis (ME). However, all these names mean the same thing — CFIDS.

Michelle Akers suffers from CFIDS. And her journey to full understanding of the illness is documented throughout the chapters of this book. At first, Michelle was told she had mono. Then she was told she had the Epstein-Barr Virus, which causes mono. Later, Michelle was found to have Chronic Fatigue Immune Dysfunction Syndrome. Throughout this book, Chronic Fatigue Immune Dysfunction Syndrome is referred to as Epstein-Barr Virus, Chronic Epstein-Barr, CFS and mono. While CFIDS is the accurate name for Michelle's illness, references to the other names for the illness remain in the book to illustrate the conflicting opinions Michelle received from various doctors and to reflect her confusion as she struggled to understand her illness. *(For more information on CFIDS, see appendix B.)*

*Michelle with Mia Hamm (left) and Julie Foudy (right) on
the gold medal platform.*

Photo by Perry McIntyre

Chapter One

MICHELLE AKERS STOOD WITH HER TEAMMATES, exhausted, not yet fully aware of what she had accomplished. Once widely recognized as the greatest women's soccer player in the world, Michelle now perhaps would be viewed as the bravest. She stood with her teammates, friends and companions for so long as they celebrated, hugged and cried. She listened to the national anthem being played, and smiled broadly as Juan Antonio Samarach gently hung a gold medal around her neck. For Michelle, that was it. Her struggle was finally over. The challenge was met with resounding valor and grace.

Five games. That was all it took. Five games represented a minuscule fraction of the one-hundred and nine international matches Michelle had played in her soccer career. There were matches that seemed more important at the time. There was the 1991 World Cup, where her goal two minutes before overtime, her tenth and final goal of the six-game tournament, gave the USA the title. There was the 1995 World Cup, perhaps the most disappointing experience of her life. And there were others, but nothing could measure up to the magnitude and significant of these five games — Denmark, Sweden, China, Norway and China again. These five games were Olympic Games. These five games signified the arrival of women's soccer in the world and in America, something on which Michelle had worked long and hard. As she stood on the medal stand basking in the drama and excitement of the moment, Michelle could not possibly fathom the significance of it all. All she could do was enjoy it the best her body would allow.

When Michelle and her teammates took the field on July 21, 1996, for their Olympic-opener with Denmark, the Citrus Bowl in Orlando, Fla., rocked with support for the Americans. The attendance of twenty-five thousand was some sixteen thousand more than the record for the largest crowd to ever watch the U.S. Women's National Soccer Team play a home game. That Michelle was able to even take the field was a miracle in itself. Suffering from Chronic Fatigue Immune Dysfunction Syndrome since 1993, Michelle fought a daily battle just to get out of bed. Some days were better than others, but none were all that great. Forcing herself, driving herself, to beat the illness — at first ignoring it, and later accepting the consequences of living with it on her own terms — Michelle became focused on reaching her dreams of being a world champion again.

So there she was, gold medal around her neck, smile on her face, vacant look in her eyes. She had reached her goal — Olympic Gold Medalist. Her struggle was over ... for now. There would still be the aftermath, the price she always had to pay for driving her body past the point of exhaustion. There would be tomorrow, like so many other days-after, when she knew she would not be able to function like a normal human being. She knew she would have to drag herself out of bed, suffer through the migraine headache she knew she would have and muddle through the day as best she could. She knew she would be back in bed by nine p.m., or earlier, fight through the insomnia and be up again before six. But all that didn't matter now.

She stood with her teammates, the people who had meant so much to her for the past ten years. They were among the few people who came closest to understanding what she went through to get here. They understood the rare occasions when Michelle didn't make it to practice, and they made a point of checking on her. They would carry her bags on the bad days when games and travel wiped her out to the point where she could barely walk. Only a few — the ones closest to her — understood how bad it really was because they had seen her at her best. They knew her as being relentless in her own training and rehabilitation. They knew she worked as hard or harder than anyone who had ever worn the USA jersey. They had seen her on the field when they got to practice and they had seen her still there when they left. Her training regimen was legendary.

Her coach, Tony DiCicco, knew too. And if Michelle Akers was healthy enough to play in the Olympics, she would be on the field. It was as simple as that. There were doubts that her health would allow her to play, though. She started the Denmark game in her normal striker position, teaming with Mia Hamm and Tiffeny Milbrett to pester the Danes. Five minutes before halftime and with the U.S. holding a 1-0 lead, Michelle had a conversation with Mia prior to a Denmark goal kick. Michelle told Mia that if the goal kick came anywhere near her, she was going to head it back toward the Denmark goal as hard as she could. "'Mia, pinch in,' she kept telling me because I was too wide," says Hamm. "'Pinch in to the middle,' she said. As soon as I moved in, she headed it back in and I had a clear path to the goal. If she hadn't told me to move, I never would have scored that goal. If it's a header, I'm putting all my money — and all the other team's money — on Michelle. And it's usually going to go a good distance." Mia, who over the years had learned to trust Michelle's instincts, gave the USA a 2-0 lead. With less than ten minutes remaining and the game well in hand, Tony DiCicco subbed Michelle out of the game. It would be the last rest she got.

Two days later, Michelle would be battered and bruised in a physical 2-1 win over Sweden, a game that required a full ninety minutes of effort. With just two days rest, which included traveling from Orlando to Miami (travel, no matter how short the trip, always played havoc with her sensitive condition), Michelle played another grueling ninety minutes in a scoreless tie with China. With the first round completed, the USA, which finished second to China in their group, advanced to the semifinals in Athens, Ga., to meet Norway. The Norwegians are the Americans' biggest rivals. In 1991, it was Michelle's goal, her second of the game, that beat Norway for the first-ever Women's World Championship. In 1995, with Michelle playing on a gimpy knee in her only full game of the world championship tournament, the Norwegians eliminated the USA 1-0. This time around, the entire U.S. team was looking to avenge that loss. It was determined long before the

Olympics that Norway and China were the two biggest obstacles standing between the Americans and Olympic gold.

With the U.S. trailing 1-0 midway through the second half, a Norway player was whistled for a hand ball in her own penalty area. A penalty kick was awarded to the Americans. Michelle, nearly out of energy, blasted it past the Norwegian goalkeeper to tie the game 1-1. Regulation time would end with the score still tied at one each. When the team huddled around their coaches for pre-overtime instructions, Michelle was flat on her back in the middle of the huddle, exhausted and doubting her ability to continue. Her friends helped her up, and she continued. Barely nine minutes into overtime, Shannon MacMillan's dramatic goal ended the game.

"What a relief," was Michelle's first thought. "Thank God, now I can rest." Then it dawned on her — they were going to play for the gold. Visibly wiped out, Michelle could do little else but head off the field. She couldn't even pause for long to wave to the crowd as she walked off, something in which she had taken great joy after the previous three games. Steve Slain, the team's trainer and Michelle's long-time friend, whisked her to the locker room and stabbed her with the first of two IV needles to begin the long process of preparing her for the gold medal match with China.

She was ready for China. But if one team was able to physically exhaust the Americans, it was the Chinese. Their team defense was stifling. There always seemed to be a dozen or so red shirts surrounding the ball. And they moved the ball so quickly and so proficiently the U.S. found themselves in the unenviable position of chasing. Michelle knew this would happen, and she knew she would have to be very careful with her energy level. She also knew this was it. The last game. After the game, she could take her gold medal and go on the vacation for which she longed.

Michelle, in a revamped lineup, was placed in center midfield with Tisha Venturini. Kristine Lilly would be on Michelle's left and Julie Foudy would be on her right. In front of her would be Tiffeny Milbrett, Mia Hamm and Shannon MacMillan. Behind her, Carla Overbeck, Brandi Chastain and Joy Fawcett. Briana Scurry would be in goal again. Tony DiCicco and the staff started experimenting with Michelle in a midfield role in February of '96. The change was made for many reasons. One, at striker, she was destroyed every time she touched the ball. Too many hack-happy defenders, too many poor referees, and too many hits were taking her out of games too early and with too much frequency. The second reason was the U.S. needed to maintain possession of the ball more, and that was one of Michelle's strong points. It is easy for her to distribute and play-make. Those are her natural tendencies. She told Tony from the beginning she loved it there. The difficult part for Michelle, after so many years of phenomenal success on the field, was accepting her physical limitations. Central midfield, while not much of a tactical or technical adjustment for Michelle, actually was harder on her physically.

With twenty-six minutes left to play in the first half, Michelle showed exactly why Tony DiCicco wanted her in the center of mid field. Against the wave of Chinese pressure, it was crucial for the U.S. to move the ball quickly and accurately, changing fields with the ball often. When Tiffeny Milbrett got the ball on the right side of a crowded midfield situation, she found Michelle with a short, quick backpass. Michelle quickly turned to her left and struck a perfectly placed, perfectly paced pass right into the path of a sprinting Kristine Lilly. Kristine bolted into Chinese territory and hit a left-footed cross that was destined to land fifteen yards in front of the Chinese goal. Mia Hamm, seemingly out of nowhere, burst into the penalty box and struck the ball with her right foot before it landed. Bang! Off the left post and right to Shannon MacMillan. Shannon, who scored perhaps the most important goal in U.S. women's soccer history three days earlier, one-upped herself, poking it home — 1-0 USA.

But the Chinese came back to tie it 1-1. Their speed and deadly accurate passing caused the Americans to chase them around midfield — a nightmare for Michelle. She was at the end of her rope. Going into the game, she had very little left. In fact, by the time the game was fifteen minutes old, she felt she'd had enough. A miserable game for someone with CFIDS, she says. Her team

5

needed her, though. And after what she had gone through to get to this point, she was not going to leave easily. On the sidelines, Steve Slain and Tony DiCicco watched her closely. In the stands, her family silently urged her to dig deep and hang on. On the field, Michelle played on pure instincts and adrenaline. Her instincts told her what to do, and sheer will, faith and adrenaline enabled her to do it. She could hear very little. The voice of Julie Foudy, because hers was the most persistent, managed to make it through Michelle's "brain fog," as she called it. Foudy's encouragement and a diluted, dull roar from the crowd was about all Michelle could hear. But her mind was telling her she was almost there. They were the same words she would use to get herself home from practice on the bad days — "You're almost there. Just a little further."

With the game winding down — and Michelle scared to death of another overtime — Joy Fawcett burst down the right side of the field and placed a perfect pass across the Chinese goal to Tiffeny Milbrett. Tiffeny popped it in, and now if the USA could hold on to a 2-1 lead for the final eighteen minutes and fifty seconds they would have their gold. And if Michelle could hold on, she would have her gold, as well as win her personal struggle. Michelle finished that game strong, winning balls in the air, plugging holes, maintaining possession. As the frenzied crowd roared through the closing moments, though, Michelle was struggling. Hang on, she told herself. Just a few more minutes.

AN HOUR AND A HALF LATER, MICHELLE STOOD WITH HER teammates. In one hand, she had flowers. With the other hand she waved to the crowd. Around her neck was a shiny gold medal. Then she stopped waving and tried to focus on a section of the stands near midfield. She shaded her eyes from the glare of the stadium lights and searched for her father. "I wanted to share the moment with him," she says.

"I wanted to let him know it was his gold medal too. It was our victory. We had done it. He could rest now too. It was all worth it. He has fought so hard for me and wants so much for me that he, as well as my stepmom, have somehow become a part of my accomplishments and disappointments."

As she searched the stadium, filled to the brim with seventy-six thousand, four hundred and eighty-one chanting Americans, Michelle was in awe and disbelief of what she and her teammates had accomplished, the circumstances of their win. In particular, she was marveling at the measure and worth of her personal struggles to be a part of this experience. She was thinking, "How cool God is, and how absolutely faithful He is to those who believe, have faith." She felt humbled and empowered by the depth and awesomeness of His plans and love for her. Pretty doggone cool, she thought.

On the Gold Medal platform, Michelle searches for her dad.
Photo by Mike Stahlschmidt

Chapter Two

MY NAME IS MICHELLE AKERS. I AM FIVE-FEET, TEN-inches tall and weigh one-hundred and fifty pounds. I'm muscular. I'm tanned. I have wild, sun-bleached, curly hair. My teammates call me Mufasa from "The Lion King." I love to laugh. On vacations, I love to hike with my dad and brother in the Cascade Mountains near Seattle, Wash. I am the starting center forward for the world-class American women's soccer team. If you saw me today, you would see a healthy, physically fit, elite athlete.

But I'm not. I am sick. And I am hanging on by the very will and courage that helped me attain my status as an elite athlete. It all began in 1991 immediately after the first FIFA Women's World Soccer Championship in China. Upon my return to the U.S., I felt tired and lethargic, but thought nothing of it. My travel and career schedule was extremely hectic and demanding. I was on the road three weeks every month. In addition to the travel, I was constantly training. I mean, who wouldn't be tired? After several months, I was becoming concerned about my increasingly diminished energy levels, and I visited a doctor. And on his advice, I rested a month or so, then resumed my soccer and appearance schedule. I also visited a nutritionist, thinking it might be diet-related. But even with a diet change, the fatigue, dizziness, migraines, night sweats, Gastro-intestine upset, and metabolism problems remained. Over time, they worsened. Then in 1993, I finally collapsed during a game. My collapse led to the unmistakable conclusion that I was sick, not just tired or run down. After various tests — echocardiogram, heart stress tests, blood tests — I was diagnosed with Mononucleosis, then Chronic Epstein Barr Virus, and finally six months later in the spring of '94, Chronic Fatigue Immune Dysfunction Syndrome.

From 1992 to the end of 1995, I felt I was in Hell. At my worst, I was barely able to function or complete day-to-day activities. It was an extreme effort to do laundry, prepare a meal, or attempt the exercise bike for five minutes. Many times, just doing these small chores, knocked me out for days or weeks. At my best, I could play fifteen or twenty minutes, or if I was really lucky, I could last thirty minutes of a ninety-minute match. I could train with light-to-moderate intensity to stay in some kind of shape for the national team, and maintain a skeletal appearance schedule for my sponsor, Umbro. The repercussions were migraines and overwhelming fatigue during, and especially after, activity. They lasted for days, sometimes weeks. It was a constant trade-off. Being able to maintain my involvement in my career and in the normal world would have to be traded with feeling the devastating effects of that activity on my body. Other symptoms included neck pain, muscle and joint stiffness, water retention, fuzzy brain, loss of balance, forgetfulness, night sweats, poor sleep, GI upset, diarrhea or constipation, high or low metabolism, weight gain or loss, emotional upheaval, sugar cravings, shortness of breath, and heart palpitations.

I can honestly say these few years were pure hell for me. I struggled to get through the day or hour or minute, depending on how bad I was feeling. I desperately searched for medical answers and help, but found very little. I frequently asked myself, "What happened to that strong, dynamic, tireless Michelle Akers? Will I ever see her again? And who am I now?" I was alone. I was scared. And I was in agony.

Some days, it was all I can do just to get through the day, let alone be an elite athlete. On those days, the only way to step on the field was to stop, close my eyes, take a deep breath, and gather every ounce of strength and will, focusing solely on surviving the hour and-a-half of practice ahead of me. Most days, I survived the practice. Sometimes, I did better than survive and actually saw glimpses of the player I used to be. Those days were glorious. To feel good. To have energy. To be light on my feet and

9

strong. That's what it's supposed to be like — fun and carefree. I revel in the feeling and the gift of good health.

I've been injured quite a bit in my career. Injuries, to me, are a part of the game. Yeah, I got hurt, and okay I had surgery, and then rehab. But who really cared. Injuries were just a pit stop and nothing but a small distraction. I suspect some of them were due to being worn down, but I was beat up in every game I ever played. The majority of these injuries were from collisions and fouls. I had torn ligaments in knees, cartilage stuff, sprained ankles, head injuries, dislocated shoulder, knocked out teeth — all part of the game and part of being a goal-scorer. Nothing to write home about … anymore. I would usually call home and tell my father, "Uh Dad, I did my knee again and have surgery scheduled for blah, blah, blah date." After a while, it became pretty trivial.

This illness, this Chronic Fatigue Immune Dysfunction Syndrome, is very different. On the very bad days — the days when it is all I can do to survive — I walk off, drag myself off, the field. My legs and body feel like lead. God, they seem to weigh so much. My breathing is labored. It's all I can do to get to the locker room, change my clothes, and keep from crying in utter exhaustion and weariness. I am light-headed and shaky. My vision is blurred. My teammates ask me if I am okay. I say I'm fine. But my eyes tell the truth. They are hollow and empty, dull and lifeless. It scares me to look in the mirror when I get like this. I shake my head knowing I overdid it again. I crossed that invisible line between functioning and being very, very sick. How long would it take to recover from this one?

I slowly get to my truck and concentrate on the road, willing myself to keep moving, to not pull over and rest. "Almost there," I tell myself. "Just a few more minutes." By the time I arrive home, I leave my bags in a pile by the door and collapse on the couch. I have no energy to eat, to shower, or to call someone for help. I have migraines so bad I wish I could go to sleep and never wake up. I have severe neck pain and knots, muscle weakness, uncoordination and an upset stomach. At night I sweat so bad, I go through three T-shirts and have wet sheets and hair. I suffer through sleepless nights, and when I do sleep, I have crazy dreams. I get a lot of chest and throat colds that make me lose my voice and cough like crazy ... brain fog ... no concentration ... no short-term memory. Sheer awfulness.

I TELL YOU THESE THINGS NOT TO GAIN SYMPATHY, BUT so you too can experience a day with this illness, experience the pounding migraine headaches that can incapacitate me for days. I tell you these things so you can understand the insomnia that plagues me even though I am exhausted, the overwhelming fatigue that keeps me from going to a movie or dinner with friends because I don't have the energy to talk, sit up, or eat. And then there's the GI upset that has caused me to go on an extreme gluten-free, dairy-free, caffeine-free, sugar-free, and alcohol-free diet in hopes of finding relief or possibly a cure. And, of course, there's the "fogginess" that causes me to lose concentration, forget where I am or how to get some place that I've been a thousand times before. This illness demands attention in every detail of my life. And if I don't pay attention, it punishes me without remorse. It's a difficult experience to explain because it encompasses so much of who I am. It's awful to realize you never will be the person you were before this illness. Chronic Fatigue Immune Dysfunction Syndrome becomes who you are at times. Leaving you — the old you — a mere shadow.

I have always believed you can accomplish anything through hard work and perseverance, through dedication and commitment. This is how I became a World Champion — an Olympic athlete. But that's the irony of the illness. The harder you work, the more it drags you down, the more it disables you. It's the first time in my life I have been beaten. I cannot defeat this illness through hard work, or through pure drive and desire. I have realized it's the first time I cannot overcome on my own terms, with my own strength.

I am a fortunate CFIDS sufferer. Because I am an elite athlete, I have access to the best doctors, the best care in the United States and, therefore, the world. I have an incredible support sys-

11

tem through my team and family. My teammates force me off the field when I am pushing too hard. They drive me home when I can't make it myself. My friends pray for me daily. They encourage and lift me up when I am at the end of myself. My family, friends, coaches, and employers — the U.S. Soccer Federation and Reebok — are sympathetic and flexible, in regards to my health and limitations. They have never doubted that I am sick and not just depressed, mentally unstable, or God forbid, faking it. Yes, I have lost a lot. Yes, CFIDS is a devastating illness. And no, I am not the same person I was before I was stricken with CFIDS. And I probably will never be. But this is not a message of hopelessness or defeat. It's a story about courage, growth, and challenge. This is a story about overcoming. I have gained a lot from this illness. It's nothing that can be touched or measured. But through suffering and heartache, I have gained a strength and purpose that carries me when I cannot do it myself. I have seen I cannot do it myself. I have seen and experienced God's grace and peace only because I have been in the valley. I now know it took this long visit in the depths of this illness to open myself to a more meaningful and purposeful life.

I live by the verse in 2 Corinthians which says, "My grace is sufficient for you, for my power is made perfect in weakness. That is why, for Christ's sake, I delight in weakness, in hardship and in difficulties. For when I am weak, I am strong." Through this weakness — this illness — God's power rests in me, and I am strong. His power is made perfect in me. I will overcome but not through any effort of my own. That's the final irony. The more I struggle to save myself from this illness, the more it takes my life away. The moment I just rest — rest in the strength of God's perfect grace — is the moment I begin to overcome. It's the moment I am whole again. I have learned to accept CFIDS as an opportunity to make a difference. I have turned this weakness into a strength. And even though it is still raging inside me, I refuse to be beaten by it.

I will overcome. And I will show others how to overcome also.

Chapter Three

BOB AKERS, MICHELLE'S father describes his only daughter as a very competitive person who had a pre-disposition to be stubborn. In fact, "stubborn" was the word the family pediatrician used for her. As an infant, when Michelle awoke, the entire house became apprised of the situation immediately, her father says. Michelle's brother Michael, two years younger, was more subtle. There were early signs of Michelle's competitiveness. She showed

Michelle with her mother, Anne, and brother, Mike

remarkable determination in learning to walk. It showed on her face, and it showed in the way she kept trying until she got it right. And she absolutely hated to lose. It was obvious at an early age that she wanted to be the best in everything she did. If she was on the losing end of anything, she got angry. Once when she was eight years old, she challenged a boy to a race. When she lost, she beat him up. If she didn't win a game of checkers, she'd get mad and storm off. And early failures on the athletic fields had one of two outcomes. She would either get more determined, or go off by herself for a while to fume in private. "I'd say something like, 'Oh Michelle, what are you getting so mad about? It's just a game,'" Bob Akers says. "And she'd give me this look that said, 'How can you be so stupid?'" Phrases like, "Better luck next time," and "It's not whether you win or lose ..." were not what Michelle wanted to hear. "When my team was losing, I would either try harder, take over the game and try to win it by myself," Michelle remembers. "Or I would play as hard as I could and then get all mad and go off by myself to try and calm down. My Dad would always ask, 'Did you have fun?' And I thought, 'What a stupid question! He obviously doesn't understand sports! You play to win. And if you don't win, it's the worst feeling in the world. You failed. Winning is fun; losing is for losers.'"

Michelle didn't want to be that way. She just couldn't help herself. It took her a long time before she figured out at which times it was okay to be as competitive as she wanted. She had to learn that sometimes it's better to back off a bit for the sake of the people around her. They would benefit more, she learned, if she was less competitive. She discovered winning became less important if she was able to help the people around her grow. She learned to be more selfless and more aware of what others needed to improve, succeed, and feel good about themselves.

"Toning down my competitiveness was very difficult for me," she says. "But I eventually learned that other people are ultimately more important than winning the game. The only place I could be myself — Miss Competition — was either with the guys or with girls like me, which were few and far between. I also learned from my brother that some people play to have fun ... and that's it. Nothing more. They don't want to spend forty-five hours a week practicing to be the best. Winning just isn't everything to them. And that was okay. That didn't mean they were any less or more than I was. They just played for different reasons, and I had to learn to accept that. I eventually realized I play soccer to have fun. I learned that, yes winning is great, but losing isn't all that bad either. It's the journey that counts the most. It's the character of your preparation, your performance on the field and your conduct off the field that really matters."

Mike Akers played to win. There was no doubt about that. But he also played to have fun, and a loss didn't stick with him as long as it did Michelle. "I hated losing too," Mike says. "But I think I introduced Michelle to the fun aspects of playing. I love the overall camaraderie of playing sports, the friends you make. She taught me to put more hard work into it, and I taught her to have more fun. It was a good trade."

While Michelle learned those lessons, she still was able to maintain the personality traits that made her the best female soccer player in the world. "I think Michelle has many great qualities," says Anson Dorrance, her national team coach from 1986 to 1994. "One is her ability to take physical risks. Also, she has this great frame on which to hang a heck of an intimidating player. But she has a wonderful competitive anger that she can call on at any time. For a lot of players, it seems that they have to get kicked in the face to get fired up, or some sort of extremely emotional event has to trigger something. The great players don't need that. Michael Jordan doesn't need all that much motivation to really go after it. I believe all the great athletes have this capacity to reach down and hit a button. Michelle hit that button all the time. She had the capacity to go one-hundred percent even in the most meaningless situations. She wanted to be the best every minute of every game or every practice. That makes her incredibly unique."

Michelle's work ethic soon became the standard by which national team players were measured. "When you look at our team, she's the workaholic," says Julie Foudy, who joined the team in 1988 at age sixteen. "When I first joined the team, I remember her being out on the field before practice, and she'd be the last one to leave. That was my first impression of her. I ask kids all the time, 'Why do you think she has the hardest shot in the world? It's because she works on it all the time!' And when we are not in training camp, she is working just as hard as she did when we are in camp."

Michelle's name was easily the most recognized in American women's soccer. Players coming into the national team camp for the first time came with preconceived notions of her. "When I first joined the team, we didn't talk a lot," says Tisha Venturini, who played her first game with the team in 1992 at age nineteen. "Then I noticed how everybody picked on her and made fun of her. Foudy made fun of her all the time. Michelle played right along, laughing all the time. I had thought she was always real serious, but she was really kind of goofy with a great sense of humor."

Mary Harvey has never seen her do it, but she has heard hilarious stories about Michelle walking in her sleep. And sometimes when a group of team members are watching a movie, everyone will laugh at a certain point, and inevitably, Michelle's distinct laugh will come a good three seconds after the punch line. "She gets picked on a lot," says Harvey, a veteran of the 1991 and '95 World Cup squads and the '96 Olympic Team. "But that's because she takes it so well."

But Michelle could certainly dish it out as well as she could take it. She set up her brother when she was in Seattle playing in a celebrity indoor game as part of a nation-wide tour of soccer legends — men and women. "She had them introduce me to the crowd," Mike explains. "The announcer said, 'We have some special guests here today. We have Mike and Michelle Akers, who have combined for three hundred goals in their careers ... Michelle has two-hundred ninety-nine and Mike has the other one.'"

PARENTAL SUPPORT WAS ALWAYS A GIVEN. BOB AKERS would leave his job early, or take a long lunch to watch Michelle and Michael play sports — basketball, baseball, softball and, of course, soccer. "Now that we've grown up, we realize that he supported us one-hundred percent ... always," says Mike Akers. "He was always at our games ... in the rain with his thermos full of coffee. I think as we've grown up, we realized that he loves us unconditionally and has always been a great parent." But Bob Akers never got caught up in all the success his daughter enjoyed. He was supportive, yet strove to keep her humble. "A lot of parents will push their kids to find their niche," Bob says. "But with Michelle, we had to back off a little."

"I think her dad's her hero ... Absolutely her hero," says Lisa Gozley, Michelle's close friend since college. "I don't think she would have gotten through any of this without her dad. Ever since

I've known Mich, her dad has always been her life-support system. He's a very wise man, and I think he is the only one who really understands her. She can't fool him. He always brings her back to what's important. They have a really, really special relationship — best friends, father-daughter. When things kind of crash down around her, she always goes home. He is her hero, hands-down."

Not overtly competitive, Bob Akers competes with himself, and he likes to push himself to the limit physically. He runs marathons, hikes through the mountains and reaches the point of near-collapse before he stops — just like his daughter on the soccer field. "In a way, I remind myself of my dad," Michelle says. "I love to compete, to push. When I'm on the field, I compete against myself for perfection, for excellence, for the sheer challenge of testing myself. And the opponents are merely obstacles. It's not like I beat them when I win. It's more like I was able to face the challenge and pushed myself to the edge. I like to see if I have more drive, more determination, more willpower than they do. The thrill for me comes from finding out how much I have inside and if I have the guts to keep going when I want to quit."

Mike Akers often marvels at his father's ability to read human behavior, and he has noticed how his dad is able to get directly to the point with Michelle. "They care about the same things, and they seem to be on the same level," says Mike, an account manager for AT&T in Seattle. "She is very similar to him. He is the silent-but-deadly type. My dad and I climbed Mount Rainier and Mount Adams together. Before the climbs, he was very quiet about his training. But once we got on the mountain, he was the one leading the rope team. Michelle is the exact same way."

When Michelle was growing up, she watched her mother, Anne, do things that average women did not do, and it made her think anything was possible. Bob, Anne, Michelle and Mike moved from Santa Clara, Calif., to Seattle when Michelle was in the fourth grade. Bob Akers was working as a meat-cutter and pursuing a master's degree in psychology at night. A year later, Bob and Anne divorced, and ten-year-old Michelle was very confused. She kept

17

herself active in sports so she wouldn't have to think about her parents' divorce and what was happening in her young life. But Michelle watched as her mother became the first female firefighter in King County, which she thought was "very cool." Anne worked twenty-four-hour shifts as a firefighter, and Michelle believes that is when she first became independent and self-sufficient.

Michelle's stepmother, Sue, is also a big supporter of Michelle, and someone from whom she learned a great deal. "Sue's daughter, Shelley, played soccer and softball with me in high school," explains Michelle. "Sue also refereed a few of my youth games and knew of me. In fact, she said I was a big mouth, which was true. Sue also coached Shelley's club soccer team, and we often traveled together to tournaments. That's where my Dad and Sue met. I have always really liked and respected Sue. She always seemed to be such a cool lady — young, hip, and yet full of wisdom and maturity. There aren't many women like that. She is who she is, and she is very candid and upfront with her feelings. She has been a great friend, surrogate Mom, supporter, and role model to me over the years. I love her."

Sue Akers, Michelle's stepmother, is a friend, fan and surrogate mom.

Chapter Four

ICHELLE'S DREAM AS A LITTLE girl was to be a wide receiver for the Pittsburgh Steelers. She practiced Hail Mary catches daily with her dad and brother in the backyard and at school during recess with the guys. Then one day, her first grade teacher pulled her aside and told her "Girls don't play football." Michelle was crushed. Fortunately, with the encouragement and support of her family, Michelle continued in sports. "We always went out in the backyard and juggled or took turns

Four-year-old Michelle displays her first medal

shooting on each other," says Mike Akers. "We had a good neighborhood. It was a good group of kids that always got together and played. Michelle never hesitated to jump in and play with us. The other kids treated her just like one of the guys. The majority of them wanted her on their team, in fact. When we picked teams, she was usually the first to get picked."

Through high school, Michelle was very active in athletics. She went to Shorecrest High in Seattle and was a three-time All-America in soccer. "I went out for the high school team and made it as a freshman, but was scared to death," Michelle remembers. "For some reason, my coach didn't start me the first match — something about not wanting me to get too cocky. I thought I would be cut for sure. I wasn't, and I started at center midfield the rest of my career there. We were a good team. We won a few Metro championships, and in my last year we won the state title.

I won all the individual awards — All-America, MVP, etc. — and had no idea what any of them were, nor how it all would impact my college career. I didn't really think about it. I just played — as I still do now — oblivious to what goes on around me. I got recruited heavily at the end of my junior year and in the beginning of my senior year. I couldn't understand what all the hoopla was about. In fact, I was pretty disgusted with the whole recruiting process — a bunch of used car salesmen, I thought. I began to dread it and dodge their calls. I visited a few schools and couldn't make up my mind until I visited the University of Central Florida, and that's where I wanted to go."

Little did Michelle know that Amy Allmann, against whom she had countless battles in Seattle club soccer, was also entering UCF that year. "Amy's club team was Team adidas and my team was the Flyers," says Michelle. "Team adidas was kind of like a mixture between Felix Unger and Goliath (in the bible) and my team was a cross between Oscar Matteson and David. They had all the primo equipment and were severely disciplined. They were what we called La Machine. My team was a bunch of rag-tag wild people. I was the youngest for many years and the older players were just plain tough! Huge too. A couple of them had to be over six feet. Anyway, we always lost to La Machine in the season, but once State Finals rolled around, we always, always beat them. I have no idea why. I guess they just choked under the pressure. Amy was always in goal and I unknowingly became their target. I really had no idea who Amy was until I met her in college. And then she told me how much she hated me. I thought it was pretty funny we were roommates."

"We were enemies," says Amy, a goalkeeper who went on to join Michelle on the U.S. National Team. "Playing against her was terrible. Probably the worst part was the entire week leading up to the game. Everybody would be saying, 'We have to play Michelle Akers!' It wasn't that we were going to play the Flyers. It was we were going to play Michelle Akers. Whenever they got a free kick, the whole team would be telling me, 'Watch out! She's going to shoot it! Get ready.' I'd be like, 'No kidding. I'm doing the best I can back here.'

"Our college coach knew we were both from Seattle, and he assumed we were friends so he put us together as roommates," continues Amy. "I remember the first day I got there. I peeked in my dorm room, and there was Michelle Akers. I didn't even know she was going to UCF. I thought, 'Oh great! I have to room with her!' Then, one day, we had a 6:00 a.m. workout. On the way there, she kept saying she knew she was going to get cut. Here she was this girl everyone was calling a freshman sensation, and she was unsure if she was going to make the team. I thought that was cool. Then one night, neither one of us could sleep. It was about 3:00 a.m., and she said, 'Amy, we live in Florida! What are we doing here?' We stayed up all night talking, and I guess that's when we became friends. A lot of people, even on our college team, didn't know her that well. A lot of people were in awe of her. They would put her on a pedestal and assume she would act like a superstar athlete. But she wasn't like that at all."

In 1984, Michelle and Amy spent most of their time acting like "geeky freshmen," says Amy. They were bored, and the upper-classmen would have nothing to do with them because that would be uncool. So they were left to their own resources to entertain themselves. "Michelle had her bicycle shipped to her from Seattle, and it came in this huge bike box. Both of us could fit in the box, and we would go around campus and hide in it. We called it SWATing — "Seattle Washington Attack Team." We got so we could run by sticking our feet out the bottom, and we cut little holes in it so we could see out. We would get in it, lean it up against the wall and watch people. When they weren't looking, we'd move the box, and they'd think they were losing their minds. We'd put it next to a pay phone while some guy was saying lovey-dovey stuff to his girlfriend. It was great. And we didn't tell anybody about this. We hid our box behind this giant wall-hanging in our room. One night, it was really late and we were out in the box. We spotted one of our teammates coming out of the library so we started following her in the box. First, we'd move it just a little, and she

21

kept looking back at it. It was just like an episode of 'Gomer Pyle' or something. Then we started chasing her. She was screaming bloody murder as this box was running after her.

"She never told anyone until a couple weeks later. One day at practice, she said to the whole team, 'You guys are going to think this is weird, but one night when I was coming home from the library, this box started chasing me.' A little while later, Michelle had to give a 'How To' speech in a class. Her speech was "How to SWAT in a Bike Box." She got an F on it because the teacher said there was no way two people could fit in a bike box. So I had to come to class with her to show the teacher how we could both fit in the box. She got her grade changed."

Michelle also met Lisa Gozley at UCF — somewhat reluctantly, though — and the two formed another unlikely friendship. Gozley transferred to Central Florida from Nassau Community College on Long Island and played at UCF for two seasons. "Let me tell you how I met Goz," says Michelle. "On her recruiting trip, she knocked on my dorm room door at 3:00 a.m., because she was curious to know who I was. Three in the morning! Typical Goz. I guess she had heard about me and had to see for herself. Well, she sat on my desk chair while I laid in bed trying unsuccessfully to ignore her, and she grilled me. She made fun of me, told me I was a Leave it to Beaver, Betty Crocker Girl and that I couldn't possibly be as good as people said I was. I told her she was just a punk, cocky New Yorker. We immediately struck up a friendship, and I kicked her out of my dorm so I could go back to sleep. I haven't been able to get rid of her ever since."

Adds Lisa, "Being a New York kid, I thought she was naive and a little goofy. I didn't think a whole lot of her then. Everyone was talking about this great Michelle Akers. Here she was this goofball, and I thought, 'I'm not impressed.' And she thought I was extremely cocky — a cocky New Yorker. When we met, I was a partyer and kind of wild. She was on the other end of the spectrum, but we found the middle road and formed a friendship. For about a year, people couldn't believe we were rooming together. She went out with us sometimes, but she was always a very strong person. You couldn't convince her to go out. No meant no!

"Michelle was someone with an incredible desire to win and to be the best," continues Lisa, now head women's soccer coach at Washington State University. "She's always had that in her. But I always thought she felt she had a responsibility to carry the torch for the soccer world. I used to look at her sometimes and say, 'What's it like to be you?' I always saw all the demands made on her, and I tried to make no demands at all. That's probably why we became friends. I tried to get her to laugh a little and take her out of the soccer world from time to time. I let her have an identity outside of the one she was living with. My husband always says, 'Why don't you get Mich to come out and talk to your team.' I just laugh and say, 'She's got enough on her plate already. She doesn't need me calling her up.' It's not difficult to be Mich's friend. She's such a great person, I consider it an honor to be amongst her friends. But at the same time, you've got to understand she's not going to have much time for you. You just try to be there for her because it's important to her that you're there."

Lisa Gozley recognized Michelle's competitive streak early, but she was often amazed at how little it showed. "She always hated losing, but she kept a lot bottled up," Lisa says. "If we lost, she'd grab her bag and walk off, and you could see her sort of fighting back any kind of emotion. Or she'd go for a run ... after games. Everybody would be dead tired, and she'd say, 'I'm going for a run.' We couldn't believe it."

In 1986, Michelle's junior season and Gozley's senior year, Central Florida was 15-3-1 at the end of the regular season, ranked sixth in the country. The team gathered in the locker room to find out who they were playing in the NCAA post-season tournament. "We knew we were going to get in the tournament, it was just a matter of who we were going to play," says Gozley. "We tied North Carolina that year and had a really, really good season. It turned out we got shafted by politics and were not invited to the tournament. We were all packed and ready to go. It was a bad scene, people throwing stuff around the locker room, screaming

23

and crying. Mich never showed any emotion. She just kind of boiled quietly. We decided we were going to go to the men's game and just hang out and be miserable. Michelle said, 'I'll meet you there. I'm going for a run first.' She ran nine miles! In those days, nine miles was unheard of. She said she just felt better and better as she ran, and then she looked up and she was in Oviedo or some place."

Michelle sat out the 1985 season with a knee injury and came back in 1988 to win the first-ever Hermann Trophy for women. The Hermann Trophy is the National College Player of the Year award that had been given to men since 1967. Again, the award was nice, but all she really wanted to do was play soccer.

"I remember when she was elected captain," Lisa says. "She wanted no part of it. She wasn't comfortable talking to the team. She didn't want to be a leader. She just wanted to be left alone to do her job. She'd like to do things at her own speed. My way of getting motivated for games was to put on Led Zeppelin and blast it. She'd slip into the corner and put on her headphones and listen to Anne Murray. I'd be like, 'What are you listening to? That motivates you?' She has really developed into a whole different person. She was a terrible writer in college, and now I see something she wrote and I ask her who wrote it for her. I hear her speak in front a big groups of people, and I ask her where that came from. Michelle as a public speaker? Come on. In college, if she saw a guy she liked, she'd go hide in the bathroom and say 'Oh my God, he's here!' And I'd say, 'Well, go talk to him!'"

AS A SOPHOMORE IN COLLEGE, MICHELLE FOUND HERSELF on the inaugural U.S. Women's National Soccer Team. Her first national team game was against Italy on August 18, 1985, in Jesolo, Italy. The USA lost 1-0. It was the team's first-ever game. "I was on the first team, the first tour, first everything," she says. "It was weird. I had no idea what I was doing. Again, I was oblivious. That seems to be my motto. I was just playing soccer. I do remember the other teams being so much better, skillfully and tactically. We just chased and chased. They fouled a lot too, grabbing, punching, spitting, kicking. And, amateurs that we were, we complained to the ref and finally started getting physical ourselves only to get a few cards. It was quite an experience. But I definitely did not feel like I was playing for the USA."

In the early days of the U.S. Women's National Team, training time was sparse, travel was done on a shoestring, and accommodations often were, well ... challenging. "We only had two or three training camps a year," says Carin Gabarra, a national team veteran. "We only had a couple of tournaments a year, and we would have a training camp a week before the tournament and then go. I remember going to Italy in 1988. We flew on a cargo plane — Tower Air. We didn't know what to expect. We wondered if it would have seats. It had seats, but it was so big it took two runways to take off.

"And the first couple of times we went to China, we were among the first Americans to get into the country," adds Carin. "That was pretty strange. They told us not to wear any bright colors and not to wear shorts because all the women always wore long pants or dresses, even though it was ninety-five degrees. I mean this is a country with two million bicycles and they're all the same color. In the hotel, a couple of the bathrooms flooded, so a lot of the players had to sleep in other rooms, two to a single bed. We had running water for one hour a day, and that was your only chance for a shower. A lot of the Chinese people had never seen Americans before, and the kids were scared to death of us. We would give them balloons and food, and they were astonished. Adults would come up to us, especially the blonde players, and grab our hair. They'd yank it because they couldn't believe it was real. And there were places where we weren't allowed to take cameras. The secret service was with us the whole time, and we'd try to ditch them for fun."

Mary Harvey's first trip with the national team was in 1989 to Sardinia, Italy. Like most stories from the early days of the national team, Harvey begins, "It was beautiful, but ... kind of, well, rustic." The training field in Sardinia was made of gravel. After two workouts on the field, the team's shoes had lost all their cleats. "They looked like cycling shoes," says Harvey, a goalkeeper who obviously had other problems with the field. In the team's only full international match of 1989, Harvey helped the U.S. shutout Poland in a 0-0 tie in Sardinia.

During most all the team's travels, the biggest problem was food. The local tastes, to put it mildly, were usually not what the players were expecting. In Bulgaria, Kristine Lilly became so frustrated with the meals that were put in front of her, all she ate the entire trip was cucumbers. Some players would lose up to ten pounds on a trip. "In China, the head of our delegation told us that it was a very poor country and they were giving us the best of everything they had," says Amy Allmann. "At one banquet, we had pigeon. We had dog, snake, ox, and I think we had cat. We begged for some rice, but they said no because rice was poor people's food. There was some sort of vegetable that looked kind of familiar and it smelled okay, so the whole trip, we were eating a lot of it. It looked a little like broccoli, and it was always served cut in little pieces. Then, at one meal it wasn't cut up. Michelle cut hers and said, 'Amy, cut open your vegetable and tell me what you see.' So I cut it open and it was full of worms. We all lost it.

"We all got very good at packing food to bring with us," adds Amy. "Snickers was a sponsor so we ate a ton of Snickers bars. But after China, I don't think I've ever eaten another Snickers. We lived on Snickers, Skittles and Combos."

Chapter Five

O N NOVEMBER 17, 1991, MICHELLE AND THE U. S. Women's National Team arrived in China for the first-ever FIFA Women's World Championships. In its six-year history, the U.S. had played fifty-two international matches, and Michelle had played in forty. In those forty games, Michelle had scored an amazing forty-two goals.

Even more mind-boggling was that thirty-six of those goals came in a twenty-eight game span that covered the four months leading up to the 1991 World Cup. Michelle should have been the most feared striker in the world. Other countries were aware of her, but they had no idea what they were in for. "Back in 1991, no one thought of the United States as a soccer power," remembers Carla Overbeck, the USA's captain and a veteran of over one-hundred international matches. "They would laugh at us ... until they saw us play. But as a team, we were very naive. We had no idea what to expect. No one really knew. I remember Michelle was like our secret weapon. It was amazing how dominant she and Carin Gabarra (then Carin Jennings) were. I don't think people knew much about the United States or our front-runners. But after that tournament, they knew. Mich was such a force."

The USA's secret weapon was scoreless in the first match of the 1991 World Cup, a 3-2 win over Sweden. Gabarra scored twice and a nineteen-year-old Mia Hamm scored the other. Two days later, in a 5-0 rout of Brazil, Michelle got her first goal of the tournament. Then two days later, she scored two more in a 3-0 win over Japan. Gaining momentum with each game, Michelle was ready to explode. The Taiwanese happened to be in the wrong place at the wrong time. In a 7-0 rout, Julie Foudy scored one

A world champion. Michelle hoists the 1991 World Cup Trophy.

Photo by Phil Stephens

goal, and Joy Fawcett (then Joy Biefeld) also scored once. Michelle got the other five goals that day. The USA's next foe for the semi-finals was Germany, and they had been paying attention. By being overly concerned with Michelle, the Germans found out the USA was a team of many weapons. Gabarra scored three times and April Heinrichs scored twice in a 5-2 win that set up the title match with Norway. On November 30, in front of sixty-five thousand people in Guanzhou, China, Michelle had both goals in a 2-0 win over Norway. The USA was the world champion. After the final whistle, Michelle searched the crowd and found her dad, giving him the thumbs up and beginning a long-standing family tradition.

The USA's performance startled the soccer world. The team's coach, Anson Dorrance, spent much of his post-game press conferences trying to convince the foreign media that these were American players who were developed in the United States, not in a foreign country or in a foreign league. After the USA trounced Brazil, whose men's teams have long been considered a collection of the most crowd-pleasing players in the world, the Brazilian coach declared that "the team that played most like Brazil today was the Americans." No one would believe that Americans could play soccer as well as this team did. At the crux of the confusion was Michelle Akers. Ten goals in six games against the best competition the world had to offer ... by an American? It's not possible, they thought.

"Just to make the level of her performance even more scary," says Dorrance, "when she overwhelmed everyone in 1991, that wasn't even Michelle Akers at her best. And she still scored ten goals. It was extraordinary. And the quality of her goals was remarkable. In China in 1991, believe it or not, Michelle was not one-hundred percent. She had slid into a sprinkler head in a training session in August and tore up her knee cap. I would say she was at eighty-five to ninety percent. The intimidating quality she brought to the game was something other teams couldn't handle. Not just because she scored goals, but the way she scored them and the way she went after balls in the air. Every single head ball that was anywhere near her, she was going to win. The first goal she scored against Norway was a perfect example. She was being marked by probably the second greatest header in the world, Heidi Store. When you watch the replay, you see Michelle jumping up over everyone and heading it so hard the goalkeeper, literally, does not move when the ball is going into the net.

"I don't think people who see her now appreciate how she intimidated and dominated everyone," continues Dorrance. "Teams set their defenses up to stop her, and she received more physical abuse than any player I've ever coached. And she was less protected by the official than any player in the world. The referees didn't feel like they had to protect Michelle because she was so strong and she didn't complain. And we were very naive. None of our players would get clipped and roll for five or ten yards like a lot of players on the other teams, who did it out of an instinct for self-protection. When Michelle got fouled, she would get up immediately, pretending nothing bothered her — which I thought was very noble. As a result, though, the referees had no compassion for her. The toll this sort of abuse has taken on her body is immense. I'm sure when she gets up in the morning, every joint in her body creaks.

"I remember when I first started coaching her, I was so afraid she would get injured, I started talking to her about tactical agility. How I defined tactical agility was to let Michelle know that if her team was winning by six goals and there was a ball rolling out of bounds and the other team's sweeper was about to boot it out of the stadium, she didn't have to go busting in there and try to keep it in bounds. It just didn't matter. But because Michelle never backed down, she would put her body at risk for a meaningless ball in a meaningless game with the result already determined. I just couldn't get her to be more careful. However, as a coach it was one of those wonderful problems. Isn't it great when a player you are coaching lists their greatest flaws as 'I take too many physical risks and I'm too aggressive!' What a great player you have on your hands, and that's what I had with Michelle."

Newspapers around the world ran prominent articles about the 1991 world title, complete with large photos and banner headlines. But in the United States, things were much, much quieter.

On the flight home, Michelle sat next to an elderly woman who asked Michelle where she was coming from.

"I was in China representing the United States in the first-ever women's world soccer championship," Michelle said proudly.

"How did you do?" the woman asked.

"We won!" Michelle exclaimed.

"That's nice," the woman said.

When the team finally arrived at JFK airport, four people were there to greet them. When twenty-year-old Julie Foudy returned to school at Stanford University, her classmates wondered where she had been. "I was in China winning the world soccer championship," Foudy told them. "Great!" they said. "Did you study for the chemistry test?" The team was stung by the lack of appreciation from their own country. However, progress was being made within the American soccer community. After the USA won the 1991 World Cup qualifying tourney in Haiti, Michelle was invited to a Soccer Industry Council of America meeting at the Sporting Goods Manufacturers of America Convention. It was the first time a female player was ever invited to speak at the meeting. She left directly from Haiti to the big-wig dinner with no idea what was expected of her.

"I got up and told them about the tournament and the upcoming '91 World Cup and what it was like to play for our team," Michelle remembers. "I told them how we had all been fired from our jobs, and I told them all we made was ten dollars a day for per diem and we needed monetary support. I remember Alan Rothenberg, the president of the United States Soccer Federation, just looking at me. I had no idea who he was at the time. I just knew we needed some help. These people were in the industry and had the bucks to do it. After the dinner, Mick Hoban from Umbro approached me. He gave me his card and said he'd call me later to discuss business. Cool, I thought."

Mick Hoban remembers Michelle's speech being a bit raw and unpolished, but he also remembers it as a very impassioned plea, coming straight from her heart. He could tell right away it was real. "Mick returned from a business trip in Phoenix and asked me about Michelle Akers," remembers Eva Ferara, who was working for Umbro at the time and later became Michelle's business manager. "I said, 'She's the best female soccer player the U.S. has!' Mick said he wanted to work out an endorsement deal with her, and I was thrilled. At Umbro, I worked with a great bunch of guys that all played soccer in college or beyond. At times, it was hard for them to think about a female playing soccer. Michelle was going to be my answer to this problem. She was a hard sell, but thanks to Mick, it happened."

Umbro flew Michelle from a soccer camp at Evergreen State College in Olympia, Wash., to Asheville, N.C., for the company's annual sales meeting with hopes of signing her to an endorsement contract. The affair was formal, and at the soccer camp Michelle didn't have any dress clothes, so she had to order a suit from Victoria's Secret. Everything went well. Michelle, her knees knocking with nervousness, met Pele, her idol. And she looked fabulous in her brand new orange Victoria's Secret suit ... and band aids

Michelle met Pele for the first time in 1991,
when she signed an endorsement contract with Umbro.

on her feet. After signing with Umbro, Michelle had no idea what she was getting into or what was expected of her. She just thought, "Good! People are starting to notice us. Now all the other players on the team will get sponsors also."

Soon after the U.S. won the World Cup, bang! Michelle was a role model and leader for women's soccer. At the National Soccer Coaches Association of American Convention immediately after the World Cup, they gave her a microphone, pushed her out on this big stage, and said "talk to everyone." She was scared to death. Michelle walked out on stage, saw what looked like a million people — coaches, friends, players, companies — and she talked. She told them about her team, about their hardships, about the World Cup. "I did okay, but felt very weird having people listen to me about soccer," she says. "I'm just a soccer player, I thought. What do I know? Umbro forced me to realize I could make a difference for the women's game. They gave me the means to realize a dream. They made it real. So I took on the role as a leader for women's soccer."

Michelle took her new role very seriously and eventually opened the door for others to sign endorsement contracts. Five years later, all the non-collegiate players on the 1996 Olympic team were under contract with either Nike, adidas, diadora, Umbro or Reebok, which sponsored Michelle and Julie Foudy. Michelle paved the way for her teammates to earn a living by treating her deal with Umbro as a job and giving it as much attention as she did anything else in her life that she deemed important. "She was new to the business side of things," says Mick Hoban. "But we helped her see the opportunity for women's soccer and for herself. The connection between the young girls and Michelle was something I had never seen before. Young girls had an absolute adulation for her. They finally had a hero of their own. She soon took it upon herself to fight for resources and recognition for the women's game. She became the point person, the crusader for women's soccer, and you could see her grow as a public person. Eva and some of our promotions people helped her with her public speaking, and she became very good at it."

Mick Hoban had never seen anyone conduct themselves more professionally than Michelle. "She was absolutely, singularly focused on her job," says Mick. "But she did it without any sense of arrogance. Being the dominant player in the game, she fully understood what she represented, and she never used it for her own personal betterment. She was just going to drag the sport along with her. I had never been around anyone like that before."

Eva Ferara discovered quickly that Michelle was serious about her new role. "I was given the task of getting the Michelle Program blended into our existing promotional campaign," explains Eva. "She put as much time in her off-field efforts as she did in her on-field work. She spent hours preparing her sessions and always had handouts and videos with her. At first, we just did grass roots clinics, and very successful ones. At one in California, we had three hundred girls and boys show up to see Michelle. She would do a session and then sign autographs. I noticed how people hung on her every word. She had an aura about her that drew people to her. But she just saw herself as a soccer player. That's all."

Just as Michelle started sinking her teeth into her new job, she started to get sick. At one clinic in St. Louis, Eva remembers having to stop three times to pump Michelle full of Pepto-Bismol and watch her struggle through the day before taking her back to the hotel and pouring her into bed. With her energy level quickly being depleted, there were times when Michelle could not perform all of her duties for Umbro, and people began to wonder why. She had set the standard with her early exuberance, and now she was not living up to her own example. She had a hard time saying no, and as a result she would over-extend herself in other projects. Sometimes her Umbro duties would suffer the consequences of CFIDS. "No one really understood the depth of her sickness," says Eva. "Many times at Umbro, I had to fight for her. The guys couldn't understand why she just didn't suck it up and do it. At times, I also didn't understand why she couldn't just squeeze in one more day or one more hour for Umbro." Caught in the middle, Eva tried to keep the relationship between Umbro and Michelle running smoothly. She told both sides only what they needed to know.

Both parties groaned about the other, so Eva absorbed the criticism herself.

But Michelle, as is her stubborn nature, didn't want to complain or give excuses. She would work it out herself, she thought. She could handle it. "When she got sick, I was real worried about her," says Lisa Gozley. "She was always jumping on a plane and going here and there. I would ask her, 'Do you ever take time just for yourself?' But she was so empowered by her role for women's soccer, she felt she was the only one who could do it, and she didn't want to let anyone down. But should she sacrifice her life for it?"

Chapter Six

I N LATE 1993, MICHELLE COLLAPSED DURING A MATCH AT the Olympic Sports Festival in San Antonio, and soon after she was diagnosed with the Epstein-Barr Virus. At first, Michelle thought she had mono. No big deal. Her understanding was that if she rested for a period of time, she would be okay. So Michelle rested for a month or so, and jumped back into activity. "Then, bam! I was out again," Michelle explains. "When I was diagnosed with Epstein-Barr Virus, I took it to mean just a more serious form of Mono. And of course, I thought, 'I can overcome this. I am tougher than this. It's just mind over matter.' I tried to ignore it away, tried to outlast it, overcome it through my own will and determination."

After more tests, the doctors told Michelle she had Chronic Fatigue Immune Dysfunction Syndrome. The illness changed her in many ways. "It changed who I was, how I was perceived, and, of course, how I functioned," she says. "The first way it changed me was, obviously, in my physical limitations, which everyone noticed. There were various levels of awareness in this area and for lots of reasons. One, because the national team didn't have much of a budget, we trained on our own for many years. No one on the team was really aware of how much I trained or to what degree. I knew I spent more time training, lifting, doing fitness, and planning my workouts than anyone else on the team, although I would have never said that publicly. So when we got together in Florida for our first-ever residential training camp prior to the '95 World Cup, people noticed each others training habits — who spent the most hours training and what they did individually. Well, Julie Foudy commented that she didn't realize how much I trained, how much extra I did before and after practice. I was sick when she said that. As we went along with our full-time training, it became obvious that I couldn't continue the way I trained before the illness. I had to make some changes. I began to do just what the team did and sometimes less, depending on how I felt. When I did less, I know people noticed because I obviously had to sit out or stop in the midst of fitness training and some practices. I was also injured a lot — approximately half the time in the 1996 training period — and I not only watched or participated in every possible practice and lifted weights, I did one-to-four hours of rehabilitation daily. Not many people knew that when I wasn't at practice, I was at rehab working my butt off for two-to-four hours. It was only on the really bad days that I did nothing or didn't show up for practice, and I have no idea if any of the rookies even noticed. I know Foudy, Carla Overbeck, Kristine Lilly, and the veterans were aware of my absence. They usually called to check up on me. So I managed to do a lot, although the cost to participate or appear normal was very high at times.

"The second big change was in my personality, which only those close to me could distinguish," she adds. "Before I got sick, I think I was untouchable in a way. I was nice. I had friends, but I was very aloof. A loner. And I still am, but to a lesser degree. When I got sick, that aloofness continued on an even deeper level. I withdrew because, in short, I felt horrible. When you don't feel well, you just want to lay down and be alone. So what I did was play soccer — where I was gregarious up to a point, and half of that was forced. Then when practice ended, I left. I went home or to my hotel room to die while everyone else hung out or whatever. Mentally, whether I was sick or not, I still pushed. I never gave in. That part of me never changed. I was always forcing myself to keep going, even to the point where someone had to tell me to get off the field. And thank God I had, and still have, that drive because it takes that kind of determination, that will and desire, just to get through the day sometimes. I needed it just to survive the one-and-half hours of practice, or on very bad days, to just survive the day. To get through the day, while I laid flat on my back sick as a dog, took every ounce of will.

Sometimes I had to force myself just to drive to practice. It all took a supreme effort some days. And when Tony DiCicco called team meetings after practice ... forget it. I could barely pay attention. It was almost too much. Many times, I'd have to stand up during the meeting to stay awake or concentrate. Sometimes, Amanda Cromwell came home with me after practice, and I would just drop on the couch. She would fix me something to eat because I just couldn't manage. Any of the extra team stuff, like dinners, fun events, team building stuff ... I probably made half at the most. Those extras usually wiped me out, or I just sat there because I didn't have the energy to participate. But I went because it was important for the whole team to be there together. It got to the point where I would ask Tony if he really wanted me there because I needed to rest more than the team bonding thing was going to benefit me or the team.

"I didn't go to the White House on several occasions with my team because resting was more important. I didn't do a lot of autograph stuff or team appearances because I needed to rest or felt too sick ... the stories are endless.

Chapter Seven

I N 1994, MICHELLE WAS UNAWARE HOW TO DEAL WITH HER
sickness. It seemed beyond her control. Nothing she did would
help, and she couldn't treat the illness the way she did the many
injuries she suffered in her career. "She couldn't say, 'This is what
I have, this is how it's cured, this is how I'm going to do it, and this
is when I'm going to be better,'" says Lisa Gozley. "Mich needs
absolutes. She's always been the type of person who says, 'What's
the problem? What's the solution? Okay, I'll do it.' That's what her
whole life has been — one challenge after another."

Michelle was confused by the original diagnosis and frustrated
by her inability to rid herself of the symptoms. "When the symptoms persisted and eventually got worse, I went back and the
doctors revised it to Chronic Epstein-Barr Virus — or CFIDS,"
says Michelle. "I was elated to have an answer. The doctor just
told me to rest, wait it out and I would eventually pull out of it. I
realize now that, although he meant well, he didn't really know
the ins and outs of CFIDS. So he told me what most doctors say
— rest and you'll recover. He made it seem almost trivial — 'Yeah
it's annoying, and you'll feel sick, but your body will pull out of it
given time.' So I figured, I'd just ease off a bit in training and walk
the fine line as I had with so many injuries. I wouldn't miss a
beat, I thought. I reasoned I could still train, push myself up to
the boundaries of the illness, and I would be fine. I had absolutely no idea what I was in for. As the months passed and I was
getting worse instead of better, I started reading bits and pieces
about CFIDS, but believed that the debilitation and limits of the
illness couldn't possibly apply to me. 'I'm different,' I thought. 'I'm
strong. I can simply will it away or will myself past it.'

"As I slowly began to approach a real understanding of the limitations and my inability to overcome, I chose simply to ignore it," Michelle explains. "It was too horrible to even let become a coherent thought. It became this abstract monster in the depths of my mind. I knew it was there, but I was far too afraid to even take a fleeting glance. It was better just to keep my hands over my eyes and pretend it wasn't there. I absolutely could not face the fact that I might not be able to play soccer. But in the far, far reaches of my mind, it wasn't so much the soccer. I was scared to death I might not ever recover, period. I might not ever be able to be active, and I would forever face the reality of suffering the symptoms of CFIDS on a daily basis, of being out of control of my life and my destiny. I was afraid of realizing I had put my life into soccer and it had failed me. And then what?

At that time, I simply chose to ignore those issues and just plow through it and push on. So I fought the illness with my every breath in order to maintain — or salvage — everything I had worked for and believed was important. I viewed CFIDS as a thief — yanking, grabbing, and slowly stealing all I owned. And I was resisting and hanging on with all of my strength and power. I focused on survival, the survival of the Michelle Akers I had built and had come to believe in beyond question. It took the slow patience and persistence of CFIDS, the wear and tear of the national team schedule, problems and conflict with Umbro, and my divorce to finally break me. I could fight the illness, I could hang on and play soccer, I could fight Umbro, but when my personal life became a shambles too, that was it. I had no respite. No place to hide. I couldn't ignore things anymore, so instead of trying to plow through it, I faced everything ... one at a time. First, my marriage, then myself — and that's an ongoing process — then the illness, then soccer. When I was in the Cascade Mountains in September of 1994, I realized I had to face everything. That was the moment I decided to let God handle it. It was just way too big for me. I didn't know where to begin. God showed me first that my person was askew. I had put my faith and efforts and focus into something empty. None of what I had worked so hard for was going to help me now. And if I wanted to fix my life, I had to decide what was the most important. I chose Christ.

AFTER MICHELLE REACHED SOME DIFFICULT CONCLUSIONS, she set her sights on her next goal — the 1995 Women's World Cup in Sweden. She focused on little else. Her daily routine — her training, her diet, her life — revolved around preparing herself to repeat her incredible 1991 performance and help her team to another world championship. But her illness was getting in the way, annoying her to no end. Everyday she thought, "I can't wait to feel good again," all the while confident the CFIDS would just go away. Here is what Michelle wrote in her journal at the time.

June 27, 1994

I'm focusing on getting ready for the 1995 World Cup in Sweden, where we will defend our world title. I had an awesome experience during the men's World Cup game in Orlando, and it made me excited for our own tournament in Sweden. I got to run out on the field holding the men's trophy. I kissed it a couple of times, waved to the crowd and pretended I was a world champion again. Surprisingly, a lot of people recognized me at the World Cup games. It feels good that all the hard work is paying off, but my dad must think it's weird. I think it must be strange for him or any close friend or family member to see me at "my job," making speeches, signing autographs, etc. I'm just Michelle to them. Nothing more. And to the public, I'm somebody famous. It was weird at first to have my family there and have the public going crazy for autographs.

IN 1994, THE MEN'S WORLD CUP OFFERED NUMEROUS opportunities for Michelle. Soccer was the main event in the United States for the first time ever, and Michelle was in demand.

There were parades, appearances for Umbro, receptions for dignitaries, travel, more appearances, more parties and more travel. Michelle's celebrity status, however, was somewhat amusing to her family and close friends.

"It's interesting, when I was in college, I was into my own thing, and I didn't really grasp how big she had become," says Mike Akers. "She was just my sister. Then I realized she was the premier women's soccer player in the world. It was amazing how many people knew my sister. At first it was strange, because when my dad and I visit Michelle, we pick on her a lot. We gang up on her, take her to the ground and tickle her. Michelle is very ticklish, and we absolutely torture her. Then later, she will be speaking to thousands of people, and they will be hanging on her every word. She handles it very well, but that's not really surprising to me. Michelle never changed who she was. She's never changed her basic values. She has always been very gracious and honest, very grounded. To this day, I still play soccer with the same group of guys I played with in high school, and when she's in town she'll come out and play with us."

Adds Lisa Gozley, "Everybody always asks what she's like. They always expect her to be really intense. Well, she's a complete goofball. She has a great sense of humor, and she's kind of an airhead. Underneath it all is a heart of gold. It's funny to see how people respond to her. Two of my players in college had to do a paper, and they wanted to do it on the women's national team, so I said, 'Let's call Michelle.' I put Mich on the speaker phone, and they just sat there looking at each other. They couldn't speak. Michelle was like, 'Hello ... Hello.' Finally one of them said, 'Um ... Hi. I'm a really big fan.'"

The attention, while surprising, was nice to Michelle. All her hard work was beginning to show. But she was not prepared for the toll all of it would take on her body. In conjunction with all the festivities of the men's World Cup, there was the business of training for an up-coming tournament of her own. The Chiquita Cup, to be held in three U.S. cities, would pit the USA against the world's top competition. After that, it was off to Montreal for the regional qualifying tournament for the 1995 Women's World Cup to be held in Sweden. She trained like always — hard, very hard. "At the time, I was training her," says Steve Slain. "I'd work her hard in the mornings and if it looked like she was too worn out at the end of the morning session, I'd say, 'Let's take the rest of the day off.' But she would go out, presumably without my knowing about it, and work just as hard that afternoon. The next day, she would be dragging. She finally admitted it when we were doing an interview for an article in Sports Illustrated. I just laughed and said, 'What do you think, I'm stupid?'"

July 5, 1994

My training is good. Steve Slain is my new running partner, and he really makes me work. It makes it a little more competitive and challenging for me. Steve also is getting on me about strength-training my legs more, so I started to put a little more emphasis on that. The Epstein-Barr is still there, but it seems to have leveled off. I just hope I can make it through the next two months and not make things worse.

DOCTOR DOUG BROWN HAD EXPLAINED TO MICHELLE THE notion that the body is connected to the mind. She had always thought the two were separate. "One lady in the book he gave me got migraines that disabled her for days," remembers Michelle. "This woman 'cured' herself through relaxation techniques and meditation. She had to learn to slow down physically and mentally in order to defeat these migraines. Through the migraines, her body was forcing her to stop, so she started listening to her body and voila. No more migraines. Sounds good, I thought. I also had terrible migraines, so I started to give myself a mental body check in the mornings before I jumped out of bed and into the day's activities. Now that doesn't mean I actually listened or followed through with what my body was telling me. I just started to realize I wasn't right, and the body check told me if it was going to be a hard day. So the book didn't really help, but it started me thinking and realizing that the mind and body were connected. Maybe someday I'll start listening to my body a little more."

Michelle sets very high standards for herself, and expects a great deal from each one of her performances. After she got sick, her standards and expectations were to play exactly as she had before the illness. Through her entire career, Michelle had never let any injuries get in her way, and she wasn't about to let this Epstein-Barr Virus stuff get in the way either. "Just play through it," she thought. "Just like any other obstacle." Driven by a desire to be the best in everything she puts her mind to, Michelle is one to never back off. But like many women her age, she never had a true role model in athletics. Unlike millions of women, however, she learned not to listen to the people telling her, "No! Girls can't do that." Through the actions of Michelle's mother, Anne, Michelle learned at an early age that a woman — a person — has no limitations. Michelle learned it was up to her to choose who she wanted to be and what she wanted out of life. In fact, it never occurred to Michelle that she had any kind of obstacles in her way. She literally went after what she wanted because she had the support of her family. Her Dad always supported her — whatever she was into. For the past fifteen years, he's been a very big influence on her life. He taught her about herself. He taught her to look inside, to dig and sift through herself, to confront her feelings, her experiences and people in her life. And Mike has always supported her and been very proud of his sister. Michelle knows it must have been hard for him to be in her athletic shadow at times.

"I didn't feel that way in high school at all," says Mike, who went on to play college soccer at the University of Central Florida, entering as a freshman in Michelle's junior season. "But in my freshman year in college and a little bit as a sophomore, I felt that way. My first year at UCF, our soccer media guide had my picture in it and a little paragraph about me, and my bio started with 'Brother of All-American Michelle Akers.' But as I matured, I realized that her soccer talent is like no other."

The message Michelle got from her family was always very clear — Go for it! Her motivation to be the best in the world came from knowing — absolutely believing — that if she set her mind to it, she could be the best in anything she chose. And once the USA won the 1991 World Cup and she had been named the world's best, it was a given that she would be able to maintain that level. She loved to play. She loved to train, and she felt her soccer was still improving. "What could stop me?," she reasoned. But CFIDS could stop her. And that was something she was just beginning to learn. In late July of '94, the USA played in the Chiquita Cup, hosting Germany, China and Norway, three severe tests for the team before the '95 World Cup. Michelle was determined to not only play but to make a large impact on every game.

July 15, 1994

I'm still feeling terrible. I went through a couple of really bad days, but now I'm getting back to fairly normal. I still can't do my full workouts, and I feel worse than I have in the past four months. And I don't know why. I just pray that I get through the summer with the national team and I'm able to play a whole match without killing myself. I am so sick of being sick and tired. Enough already, I learned my lesson. If only I could have some energy. It would be so great to play without this hanging over my head.

IN THE CHIQUITA CUP, THE PLAN WAS FOR MICHELLE TO gradually work her way up to a full ninety-minute game. Tony DiCicco, who took over as head coach for Anson Dorrance on the eve of the team's first match when Dorrance retired from international coaching, wanted to ease her back, let her body determine her playing time. So Michelle played sparingly in the three matches, but managed two goals. And the USA went undefeated, beating Germany 2-1, China 1-0 and Norway 4-1. Michelle had two goals.

On August 13, five days after the conclusion of the Chiquita Cup, the U.S. arrived in Montreal for World Cup qualifying. No team in the region was anywhere close to a match for the talented USA team. The Americans breezed through the qualifying tournament, outscoring their four opponents 36-1. Michelle scored six times. The U.S. beat Canada 6-0 in the final game of the qualifying tournament, and Michelle was named the tournament's Most Valuable Player, an award she felt she did not deserve because of her limited time on the field. She felt she won the award based on her reputation. She accepted the trophy gracefully, but was not happy about it. Her play didn't live up to her standards so she was not satisfied, MVP or no MVP. After the tournament ended, the Mexican and Trinidad & Tobago teams had their pictures taken with her, and it hit her that it was all over. She could rest. Suffering from migraines and fatigue from the summer's activities and mentally exhausted from struggling all the time, Michelle headed to Seattle to distance herself from her struggles.

Chapter Eight

SEPTEMBER, 1994: MICHELLE WAS UNDERGOING SOME serious changes in her life. She was coming to the unmistakable conclusion that she would have to live with the effects of her illness, and it was going to change her life drastically. On September 12, she finally made it home to Seattle, her spot of refuge, for her long-anticipated vacation.

After a year of trying to battle the virus and still maintain her career and four-year-old marriage, Michelle hit rock bottom emotionally, physically and spiritually. She had become a Christian in high school, but had thrown any obedience or relationship with God out the window when her life turned around and things began rolling her way — full college scholarship, success in her career, friends, travel, money, husband. For ten years, she followed her instincts, her rules and her desires. Now, she was depressed, sick, alone and empty. After realizing the pathetic state of her life, she established priorities. Michelle left for the Cascade Mountains in hopes of remembering or rediscovering who she was and what was important to her. In the Cascades, she gave her life back to Jesus.

"The cool thing is when I chose Christ, I was immediately rewarded with what I call a vision, which shows me in retrospect how so very personal God is," Michelle explains. "I am a very goal-oriented person. I have to see where I am going, what I am working toward, before I can really go after something. Well, that's when God, through an experience at my grandparent's church, showed me what He wanted me to do for Him. He scared the absolute heck out of me because it was bigger and more important than anything I had ever considered taking on. But at the same time, it showed me where I was going and what was expected of me. Later, it showed me the faith God had in me to do this for Him. It also gave me some direction, hope and purpose. He gave me what I needed to take the first step toward Him and out of the mess my life was in.

September 12, 1994

I'm still going to church and really getting a lot out of it. I went with Grandma and Grandpa yesterday, and the sermon was about this family that God called to go to Africa. They talked about being chosen and how God gave you special talents in order to let other people know about Him. The whole time, I knew he was talking to me. I tried to ignore it, but I know he was talking to me. I kept saying, "Why me? Why do you have to pick me? I want to be a normal person in one area of my life and now you have to make me different in that area too." I'm scared to death. My visions are of me speaking to churches and soccer groups around the U.S. – and maybe the world – about Christianity. I know I can do it, but it just scares me silly.

MICHELLE KNEW SHE WAS IN THE POSITION TO SERVE THIS role. But at first she was uncomfortable with it. The demands on her time and life were already more than she believed she could handle. Soccer had taken Michelle all around the world, playing in fifteen different countries. After the 1991 World Cup, opportunities for her to be a spokesperson for women's soccer presented themselves on a regular basis. In addition to her travels with the national team, Michelle received invitations to speak to various soccer federations around the world, opportunities she could not pass up. Promoting women's soccer was her job as she saw it. It was a duty, an obligation. Now, she was beginning to understand how all that fit into the plan God had mapped out for her.

As she would later discover, however, the path He had chosen for her was not smooth. She would have to accept it with grace and courage. She knew why she had been chosen. She knew God called on her to use the status He had given her, and to use it with the drive and determination needed to accomplish His plan. So at her family's cabin in Leavenworth, Wash., a gorgeous setting filled with nothing but peace and quiet, she tried to figure it all out. "In our childhood, Michelle and I went through all the divorce stuff, and we really never had any real family traditions," says her brother. "I think the cabin kind of makes up for that. It has the feel of family." The cabin was just what Michelle needed at this time in her life. Just being there made her feel better, the migraines where still there, but somehow they didn't bother her as much. "To me, the cabin represents a place of solitude and peace," Michelle explains. "It gives me a chance to be small and inconsequential. Mountains, rivers and nature tend to humble me, and I need to get back to that pretty often. It keeps me grounded." A fire had ripped through the forest two months prior to her arrival, but her family's property was untouched. The faint smell of an old campfire remained. As Michelle's place of refuge

The Akers' family cabin in Leavenworth, Wash.,
is Michelle's place of refuge.

underwent a re-birth from the fire, so did Michelle's life. On her favorite rock, Michelle vowed to give her life to Jesus.

On the second day at the cabin, Michelle embarked on an ambitious venture. She set out on a hike, intending to take a short walk through the woods. However, as she often did when something was on her mind, she ended up going sixteen miles and had to sprint the final two-hundred yards in order to get back before dark. The next day, she was suffering again. Realizing a change of scenery alone would not cure her illness, she spent the day uttering the familiar words, "I wish this would go away so I could get on with things." Her time away from the real world flew by. Before she knew it, she was headed back to Seattle, visiting with friends and family. Feeling slightly rejuvenated from the vacation, Michelle went back to work.

Chapter Nine

I N THE FIRST WEEK OF DECEMBER, 1994, THE U.S. WOMEN'S National Team opened a residential training facility in Sanford, Fla., near Michelle's home in Lake Mary. Michelle was thrilled. Having the team in Florida was an incredible boost for her. Not only did it do wonders for her personal training and preparation, it also signified a precedent-setting commitment to women's soccer by the United States Soccer Federation, a group that Michelle knocked heads with for years in her on-going efforts to promote women's soccer. A core group of players were now under contract and actually able to make a living while training for the World Cup. Four years earlier, in preparation for the 1991 World Cup in China, team members had to quit their jobs, take leaves of absence or get fired so they could put in the necessary training time. They mostly had to depend on their families for financial support and on each other for moral support. They were rewarded with a world championship that hardly anyone knew about.

Michelle's health seemed to be improving, but she had not yet completely learned about the wicked roller-coaster on which she was riding. During the periods when she felt well, she would be so thrilled about not going through the agonizing symptoms that she would push herself too far. The cycle was endless. She would feel better, then overdo it and suffer the consequences. But at this point, she had more energy than she'd had in months. And for the first time in what seemed an eternity, she was able to put on her soccer shoes and play hard. She loved it. She lifted weights, started a speed-training program and worked out with the team once a day. Things were starting to look better for her, but she felt guilty. "I didn't think about God one time out there," she lamented after one practice. "That's one thing I'll change next time. Like Dave Dravecky said, 'My only audience should be God.'"

The second week of December was an off-week for the national team, but not for Michelle.

December, 11, 1994

Saturday was the big race. Dad did a half-marathon in about two hours; Steve in about an hour and forty-five minutes. I ran the 5k. It was a hot day and I was dying. But I didn't want any kids or old women beating me. I pushed pretty hard, despite not feeling well. After the race, we went out for breakfast and did some shopping.

OF COURSE, MICHELLE SUFFERED AFTER THE RACE. AND she suffered the next day. Two days later, though, she resumed her sprint program. Michelle simply loves to train. She loves it while she is working out, and she loves it after she finishes. But it was a struggle.

"In a way, working out made me feel better. But in a way, it made me feel worse," Michelle says. "It made me feel better because I was outside in the fresh air — playing soccer, being physical, pushing myself. I was with the team, my friends, so I was not alone in my efforts. But at the same time, it was tough mentally because I still could not train as hard as I wanted. My mind and body were not responding in the way they had in the past. I was sluggish, tired, slow … sick. That was frustrating. On the field, I was not the same player. I wasn't fit, I had no endurance, and I was slow. The after-effects of the practice were extreme, sometimes laying me out for days. Plus our travel schedule was extensive. I was on one heckuva tough ride, but what did I have to lose? It was hard, but it was worth it. I knew that to quit would be ending it before it was time. I don't know how I knew this, I just did. Something kept telling me to keep going, keep fighting, and the strength would be there when I needed it."

It wasn't until later that Michelle was cautioned about the effect of exercise on someone suffering from Chronic Fatigue Immune Dysfunction Syndrome. In general, known information suggested it was very dangerous for her to be working so hard, driving her body to the point of exhaustion. But for Michelle, it was a necessity. She did, however, learn to train carefully, and that was beginning to bug her. "I hope this all clears up soon, so I can just go out and have fun again," she said time and time again. "I'm tired of watching what I do. It would be nice just to blow it out for once."

After 1994, Michelle began to see the light at the end of the tunnel. She slowly — ever so slowly — progressed to better health, or so she thought. Michelle attributes her slight recovery to a variety of things. First was a change in her eating habits. She made a conscious effort to eat a balanced diet. She ate small meals four or five times a day to maintain a steady energy supply, and she even tried various herbs, but they didn't seem to work. Rest was very, very important. Each day she took a quiet time and either slept or just closed her eyes for ten to forty-five minutes. Her body dictated how much exercise she did that day, and she listened. Rather than pushing hard every day, she went to the limit less often. Michelle also started having smarter, shorter, supervised workouts. Knowing that when she was left on her own, she absolutely could not stop her workouts before reaching the point of collapse, she hired Steve Slain as a training partner. He monitored her physical symptoms and condition daily and forced her to be accountable. They devised an exercise program to slowly get Michelle back on her feet, and they pulled back when she wasn't responding. She gradually began to see results.

Perhaps the most important factor was taking a long look at her life and career. "I learned nothing on earth is more valuable than my health, so I prioritized the things that were most important to me," Michelle explains. "I chose to focus on things that contributed to my health. For example: vacations, walks, friends, family, eating right, rest, and Christ. Those things contributed to my overall well-being and became high on my priority list. I cut out feeling anxious or guilty about not being able to exercise. I no longer stressed over errands, and I stopped rushing through my life, to name just a few. I also streamlined my career. I decided I wasn't going to kill myself for the company I worked for, and I couldn't be everywhere for everyone. I chose which things were most important to me and the company, and I concentrated on just those areas. I talked with my employer and asked them to cut my travel schedule. I said no a lot and stuck to it. I cut out everything except the most important in order to save the energy I needed to get healthy.

"Stress reduction, both emotionally and physically, was very important," she continues. "I learned we can choose how to respond to the emotions we feel. When an energy-sapping emotion flares up, like anger, anxiousness, guilt or fear, we can take hold of it and refuse to let it control or take away from the energy reserve we are trying to build or maintain. Choose to dismiss it. Choose to confront it and overcome it. It isn't easy, but it is possible. By keeping our priorities in the forefront and recognizing negative feelings early, we can head off a lot of physical repercussions that slow our recovery and sense of well-being.

"Spiritually, I rekindled my relationship with Christ. This was a major step. In fact, I will say my faith was the beginning — and is the center — of my on-going recovery. It is how I deal with CFIDS on a day-to-day basis. I think everyone who is chronically ill has been forced to take a close look at a higher power. I learned I did not have the strength to carry on under my own power. I wondered, 'What is all this for? Is there a purpose for this terrible illness and my humiliation and suffering?' I asked myself how I could possibly contribute to the world? God answered all those questions by providing the strength, courage, peace, and the people. He gave — and still gives — me everything I need to live and overcome in sickness or in health."

MICHELLE STARTED 1995 WITH A RENEWED SPIRIT. IT WAS, after all, the World Cup year, and she had it in her sights. Her game was getting better, advancing to the point where she was surprising herself with how well she was playing. She still had her bad days, but she was learning to live with the consequences.

January 1, 1995

Happy New Year!! Unbelievable. It's finally the World Cup year. I did nothing special to bring in the New Year, but this is the most excited I've been about Jan. 1 in my life. The World Cup year and the national team training down here full time. I'm very excited. I have been feeling miserable all week, and I'm just beginning to come out of it. Just in time to drive all the way to Miami, stay up late, and drive back in the morning. Oh well. I have to live sometime. Not every day can be lived for soccer. I just hope I don't lose too many days because of it. Busy week. Busy month. So let's look at what I bring with me into the New Year — new furniture on the way, a new apartment, renegotiated Umbro contract or possibly a whole new sponsor, a final divorce hearing on the 10th, dreams to move to Seattle, a happy heart, a new commitment in Christ. I can't wait for it all to happen. If it's half as challenging and exciting as this past year, I'll be blessed.

IN MID-JANUARY, MICHELLE MADE HER ANNUAL TREK TO the National Soccer Coaches Association of America Convention. The event is sponsored by Umbro, and each year Michelle makes appearances, gives speeches and demonstrations. Traditionally, the weekend is hectic, but this year it wore her down more than she anticipated. A week later, still lethargic and not feeling well at all, she traveled to Phoenix for the national team camp. The training camp was the beginning of the team's quest for its second straight world title, and Michelle wanted so badly to be a dominant force once again. She thought of the ten goals she scored in 1991, the feeling of winning a world championship and knowing she was a major part. But realistically, she had smaller goals in the back of her mind. "I hope I'm okay today," she said. "I'm really excited about the World Cup, but nervous because of my health. I hope and pray I will be able to compete and play without any physical restrictions. On the outside, I will deal with it. But on the inside, I will be heartbroken if I have to play sick or injured." The camp went well for Michelle, who turned twenty-nine years old on February 1. She was generally pleased with her overall play, and headed back to Florida to rest — a little — and to get ready for the next camp.

The national team was getting ready to resume residential training camp in Florida, and Michelle's life was changing rapidly. She was ready to become a new person, looking forward to finding the "new-old me." She could feel it happening and was welcoming it. Not apprehensive about change, Michelle was learning to accept what was happening to her.

February 5, 1995

The team is moving down here again. I can't wait to train. I just wish I was healthy. I feel like I always have to ration myself, to get through the week. I hate it. I cannot wait to do what I want, when I want. My life is changing quickly, and God is leading me somewhere. I don't know where yet, but at least now I am trying to listen and do. We'll see where it takes me.

Chapter Ten

RESIDENTIAL TRAINING CAMP GAVE MICHELLE REASON to be optimistic. She was playing better than she had in a long time, feeling good and scoring goals. Perhaps it was the new-old Michelle. Maybe she was back. She played her first full ninety-minute game in what seemed like an eternity against her old Orlando club, Calibre, scoring four times. She followed that up with another ninety-minute effort against Denmark on February 24. She scored three more goals in a 7-0 win over the Danes. The day after the Denmark game, Michelle was "foggy" and very tired, but not really sick. It was, to say the least, encouraging. Then came a large dose of realism.

February 26, 1995

I got a bunch of info from a fan about Epstein-Barr and Chronic Fatigue Syndrome. Scared the heck out of me. I didn't realize it was so debilitating and serious. The good news is that each person has their own level of tolerance and recovery rate. Looks like I might have a chance. All I can do is play and live within my limits, and not worry about the limitations of other people who have the virus. Chronic Fatigue Immune Dysfunction Syndrome is supposed to be an over-active immune system. The system overworks, causing the fatigue and other symptoms. They say the headaches come from a lack of blood flow to the brain. And it usually occurs after exercise and lasts for up to twenty-four hours. It fits with what happens to me. I still can't believe I have this illness ... of all people.

57

MICHELLE FINALLY REALIZED SHE WAS SERIOUSLY ILL. Up to this point, she had tried to downplay it in her mind. But just as she was starting to believe she would be able to play hard and play well, she now learned she would have to accept the illness as severe.

"I started reading about CFIDS and talking about it in the press, and with the interviews, fans started responding," she says. "One letter and phone call really scared me. The guy's name was Robert Montgomery. I don't know how I remember his name. He must have made a large impact on me. He told me to be careful. He said this is nothing to mess around with, that it can come back and hit you five times as hard as the initial infection. He said not to exercise. I was scared. Plus, all the literature says to avoid exercise at any level because it intensifies the symptoms. Even though I knew it to be true, I decided I would do it my way. There was no way was I going to quit. I was not about to give in to this illness."

Michelle had her faith in God on which to rest. She was becoming more and more convinced that God had a specific plan for her, and she wondered daily what it might be. Michelle realized, however, that God had put Robert Montgomery in her path for a reason. The information from him was more than a tap on the shoulder from God. It was a major nudge. And Michelle was getting the message. She was beginning to grow in many different directions and felt like her life was heading in a good direction. Slowly but surely, she thought, the Lord was putting her back together again. "I am actually happy most of the time," she said. Her faith made it easier to accept all that was happening to her. She was trying to put her life in the Lord's hands, but for Michelle, always self-sufficient and driven, it was no easy task. "I am a strong-willed, independent person who likes to be in control of my life," she explains. "It takes a two-by-four over the head to get through to me sometimes, and that's exactly what the Lord hit me with. It wasn't a punishment. It was a wake-up call. Some people take a tap on the shoulder. I take a hammer to the head. He was saying to me, 'Pay attention! This is important! You can't do it on your own. Rely on Me and I will give you what you need.'"

Having her teammates around was the perfect tonic for Michelle. There is a tight bond between players on the national team. A bystander watching as they physically beat each other senseless in training sessions would assume they are a collection of individuals who cannot stand each other. In fact, the exact opposite is true. They compete fiercely against each other. They push each other. They hammer each other. And they do all that because they genuinely love and care about each other. They are striving for a common goal, and they realize they need each and every team member to give every ounce to the cause. They won't stand for less from anyone. The relationships run very deep, and the friendships are based on a type of mutual respect that can only be earned.

"I have fun with my team most of the time, even when the trip or the experience is a nightmare," says Michelle. "Basically, I have a good time with my team as people. We get along great. We have fun together. We razz each other and laugh a lot. We aspire to be the best team in the world, and we work hard together to make each other the best on and off the field. In a way, we are sick in that we enjoy doing fitness. We enjoy pushing ourselves to the edge — that's fun to us. If it wasn't fun the majority of the time, I wouldn't be doing this and neither would they. So even though I pay a high price to play soccer, the rewards are tremendous because I am able to be around some very impressive and uplifting individuals."

Her teammates knew she was not well, but they didn't know the extent of her illness. Neither did Michelle for that matter. So they pushed her and expected her to push back. For the first time in a long time, she felt energized. The presence of her teammates in Florida represented two very important things. First, friends. Second, a constant reminder of why they were there — to win a world championship. Those feelings didn't last long, however. Suddenly, as if Michelle's life were not complicated enough, there were new setbacks.

March 2, 1995:

Unbelievable how things work out. The last couple days I have been down in the dumps. I'm concerned about my health. Not the CFIDS especially, but my body. I pulled my soleus (calf) muscle, and I'm out for a while with that. I have bruises up and down my left leg (it looks like a truck hit me), and now my shoulder is bothering me in a way that makes me nervous. I feel like I need to live in a room of pillows for a month so I can heal up and get back to training.

MORE REHAB. MORE TIME WITH NAGGING, ANNOYING injuries slowed her progress. There was so much to do, she thought, and her body was not cooperating. After a week of recuperating her calf injury, it was well enough to train hard in preparation for the Algarve Cup in Portugal in mid-March. The illness and injuries put Michelle in an unfamiliar position. Everyone else on the team, it seemed, was in better shape. She had to try to catch up, but she had to be very careful not to overdo it. The tournament in Portugal would give her a chance to get fitter. Her goals for Portugal were to play simple soccer, stay healthy and work on fitness.

Portugal was encouraging for Michelle personally. The team did not play as well as it could have, tying Norway and losing to Denmark. Michelle, however, was pleased by her overall performance. "In the first game, not only were players hanging on me and kicking me, but I was still uncoordinated from the EBV and my calf injury," she says. "But I got my spring back. I finally lost that dragging feeling." Michelle's performance in the 1991 World Cup made her a target for opponents around the world. To stop her, they had to hack her, and her shins, ankles, thighs and knees displayed the battle scars to prove it. Having survived Portugal, it was back to Florida for an abundance of doctor appointments and more training with the national team. The Portugal trip produced a slight meniscus tear in her left knee, shin hematoma, a deep thigh bruise and a hip injury. After a week of being poked, prodded, X-rayed and MRI'ed, she knew the extent of each. She was certainly battered and bruised, but no big deal. Besides, her EBV numbers were down, way down. And that was enough reason to be optimistic. That was all she was concerned about because the virus was really the only thing that could keep her from the 1995 World Cup. The other good news — no cavities.

The next trip in preparation for the World Cup was to France in April. The national team would meet Italy, Canada and France over four days, and then return home to embark on the Nike Road to Sweden Tour, a four-week jaunt which would take the team from Decatur, Ga., to Edmonton, Alberta. But first, France.

April 10, 1995:

We arrived Saturday morning, and yesterday we went into Paris for sightseeing. Then we returned home to our typical dinner of rice (or potatoes, fries) and non-distinguishable meat slub. Yuk. We are pretty much eating tons of the hard bread with Peanut Butter and jelly, creating two or three mouth lacerations per meal. The rest of the menu consists of coffee or hot chocolate, and various other U.S. food supplements — oatmeal, cereal (Lucky Charms are the hot item) and Cokes. Patty Marshak brought a trunk full of food. Thank God! We then retired to our lovely dormitory for the night (which looks like something the Jetsons would live in.) I wound up in Doc's room talking with Patty till 1:00 a.m. about life issues.

The team is sick of travel and soccer, but maintains a professional attitude of commitment and excellence. Personally, I can't wait for the World Cup. I'm sick of travel and long for a vacation in Maui. But once I get here, the competition and love for the game takes over. I just love to play. I guess I'm just tired of the process we endure — bad meals, planes, busses, feeling sick — to get to the games or training sessions.

61

THERE ARE CERTAIN PERKS THAT COME WITH BEING A WORLD champion, and for Michelle it was increased exposure. She was able to become a spokesperson for women's soccer, not only in the United States but in the world. From 1991 to 1994, she traveled extensively — Scotland, Portugal, France, Sweden and Trinidad among others. She met with various national federations and was a guest of FIFA, soccer's international governing body. She also began the arduous task of helping convince the International Olympic Committee that women's soccer should be a medal sport in the Olympics, teaming with a woman named Marilyn Childress, who had taken up the fight on her own. Michelle saw herself as an ambassador for women's soccer. Being a world champion, an honest, passionate public speaker and an elite female athlete put her in this unique position.

In the early days of the U.S. National Team, coach Anson Dorrance convinced all the players that they were salesmen for their sport. There were, he said, millions of people who had to be convinced. He told the players that every day they were in the public's eye, they should remember their responsibility to the game of women's soccer. "Anson always reminded us to 'sell' the game," Michelle remembers. "Every time we played, or met people, or did clinics, it was a chance to convert skeptic into fans. It was, and still is, difficult at times. We have to be nice to people who think we are invading their sacred sport or playing a game that only men play. There are lots of negative attitudes and criticism out there, and sometimes the old patience wears thin. I learned it was a choice. Everyday, I chose to not let them get me down. I would sell them on our game if it killed me. I just had to be patient, get them to the game, and they were all mine. I knew they would love us."

At times, however, Michelle and her teammates felt like a sideshow, especially in Europe.

April 13, 1995:

In France, people stare very openly. Mostly men, but women, too. The French and Italians just about have their jaws on the floor they stare so much. When I walked into two of our receptions, they formed a semi-circle around me and just looked. It was kind of funny. They were in part comparing my height to theirs. They're short. The other reasons ... I'm afraid to guess. I've come to call them "gawkers." They have no inhibition at all and don't look away or say hello when confronted. I don't know if they are surprised to see women in soccer gear or if they are just plain rude. But we must be a surprise to them.

MICHELLE'S TRAVELS TOOK HER TO PLACES WHERE WOMEN'S soccer was not accepted at all. While in Scotland in 1994, Michelle spoke to a group of Scottish players. She told them about the importance of training on their own away from organized camps or teams. She explained to them the commitment the members of the U.S. team have made, both personal and professional. "I remember when she was in Scotland, speaking to the group of girls who made up the Scottish National Team," says Mick Hoban. "They were probably between sixteen and twenty-five years old, tiny and pale. And there was Michelle, with what seemed to them to be a massive frame, and a tanned, chiseled body. They were in absolute awe. They looked at her like she was from another planet. But she told them, 'Yes, you can do it. You can overcome all the obstacles. No, I don't get paid to play on the national team.' She gave those girls a lot."

Michelle left feeling she had helped women's soccer in Scotland take a big step, but she was stunned by the overall chauvinistic attitude of the men in the Scottish Football Association. Still, all the attention Michelle received was a bit bewildering. In her mind, she was just a soccer player. But after she was labeled the "Best in the World," she was thrown into the role of spokesperson for the game. It became an obligation. She knew she was in the best position to make a difference, to advance the sport. But at times she felt ill-prepared.

"The respect as a superstar was surprising for me," Michelle says. "I didn't crave it or really desire it, but it was nice. It was nice to be appreciated, but I had to prove myself each and every game, and only then was I the best. It was a past-present kind of thing. If the title was based on a past tourney or the 1991 World Cup, it wasn't accurate. So the fact that these people hadn't seen me play and still gave me that kind of respect amazed me. I mean, the refs were asking me for autographs and photos. Aren't they supposed to be immune to that or something? People treated me so differently from the rest of my teammates. I was like a VIP or something, rather than just a soccer player, which is how I saw myself — just a soccer player."

When Michelle was placed in the forefront, she found herself in an awkward position with her teammates. "No one on the team had been given attention like that before, and suddenly I was thrust in the spotlight," explains Michelle. "I alone was getting all the recognition. I was playing extremely well, but the exposure I got with Umbro was incredible compared to anything we had gotten in the past. I also began wearing Umbro stuff to national team tours and other events. The team noticed. I did it for one reason only, but they interpreted it differently. They thought I was doing it to flaunt what I had — a new deal, gear, money, whatever. But I did it for them, for us. You see, The United States Soccer Federation required us to wear adidas apparel and shoes, but they made us buy it ourselves. So when I signed the contract, I showed up wearing Umbro. When the administrator told me to change into adidas, I said 'Give it to me and I'll wear it.' We soon found ourselves with adidas gear supplied to us by the Federation. The problem was the misinterpretation of my actions during that time. I was already shy, and to have them think I was a jerk and selfish, hurt. But I figured they'd get over it and we'd get what we deserved and needed."

"At first, I thought, 'Who does she think she is,'" says Kristine Lilly. "Why her? But then I realized she was using her leverage and her position to benefit us all. And she does a great job with it. It all just sort of fell into her hands, and to her credit she did it.

Autograph sessions can be time consuming and crowded,
but Michelle and her teammates try to oblige everyone.

And she did it well. I've noticed she is very cautious about what people think. I think people who don't know her too well get the impression that she is just out for herself. It's like with autographs. Michelle and Mia especially have about a hundred people waiting for their autographs after games. If they can't sign them all, the people might think they are stuck up or something. But what they don't realize is that they have to leave sometime. They can't possibly sign them all. But they both handle it very well. They're great at it."

Fortunately, Michelle was able to receive some guidance from someone she had a little in common with. "I met Pele for the first time when I signed with Umbro, and he has been an incredible influence on my career as a leader in soccer," she says. "He is always so gracious, so patient and very personable. I admire him more for this than for his soccer ability. Our relationship is full of friendship and professional admiration. I'm sure he has never met a woman like me, and he has my utmost respect and admiration as a professional."

Mick Hoban and the people at Umbro helped Michelle cultivate her relationship with Pele. "I remember talking to him saying, 'Here is someone who has as much passion for the game as you do,'" says Mick. "He sat down with her a few times in private, at dinner or in a hotel, and she would come back revitalized. She was amazed at how he always kept up such a positive public persona, how he always had time for the kids and autographs."

Personal appearances for her sponsor were an important part of Michelle's job and something she took very seriously.

Photo by Joanie Komura

Chapter Eleven

BEING IN FRANCE WITH ITS SMALL TOWNS, INTIMATE stadiums, picturesque countryside and chilly weather, reminded Michelle of the time she spent in Sweden playing professionally. She played three seasons in Sweden — 1990, 1992 and 1994. In her final season there, she was joined by USA teammates Julie Foudy, Kristine Lilly and Mary Harvey. After college, there was no place in the United States for Michelle to continue playing a high level of soccer. The United States offered very little elite competition, and none on any kind of regular basis. So Michelle and her husband Roby went to Sweden, where Michelle played and Roby coached. Sweden had always been a leader in women's soccer, making a serious commitment to the sport before most countries. Scandinavian countries had accepted females as serious athletes before most European nations, and the Swedes offered Michelle a place to play, but she made very little money. She was sponsored by local businesses — an oil company gave her a month's worth of free gas, and a restaurant provided her with one free meal a day. But she was able to play. She got regular training and regular games against good players. The training environment, however, was frustrating.

"The Swedish women's and men's teams are very team-oriented and simple," Michelle says. "Everyone has a solid technical background, and everyone is competent. They all understand the game because they have watched it and grown up with it. Everyone can do their job, and everyone pulls for the team. There aren't really any individual stars because in Sweden the team is the number-one thing. The American team is built around three or four big stars. We are team players, but we are dynamic and not afraid to step up and be different from everyone else. In Sweden, if someone scored a great goal and you told them it was a great goal, they'd say, 'No, it was lucky.' I told them, 'No, that was a great goal, say thank you.' It's just different. It was frustrating when I tried to train competitively in a Swedish practice. None of the Swedes could pick up the pace or dominate another teammate in practice for fear of making her feel bad, degraded or inferior to the winners. In a competitive environment, the Swedes would rather not stretch themselves as individuals in order to keep the whole group happy. As soon as one individual is compromised, then the others back off and stop pushing or playing hard. At one point, they had a meeting with Roby saying Lil and Foudy dribbled too much and he wasn't involving all the players in the exercises. Again, the Swedish mentality — everyone is equal and deserves the same attention and opportunity to play, no matter what the consequences to total team development. They would almost rather lose every game and have a happy team environment, than win and have the subs or B-team players feel a little left out. It was very frustrating.

"I suppose it's the same problem we have in the U.S. with no one seeing enough high-level competition. People think they don't need to make changes in training habits or game styles because they don't understand how good or how intense they must be to succeed. "

In less than two months, Michelle would be back in Sweden for the 1995 FIFA Women's World Championship. She felt she'd be ready for the World Cup, and it was an exciting time for her. She had goals in the first two games of the France trip. She played seventy minutes in each of the first two matches and lasted the full ninety minutes in the third, a 3-0 win over France. She couldn't wait for Sweden '95.

April 20, 1995:

I looked at my photo albums yesterday. I decided to keep the 1991 World Cup one out to remind me of where I want to be and how hard it was to get there. I want to be World Champion again.

Chapter Twelve

AFTER RETURNING FROM FRANCE, MICHELLE SPENT a week recuperating. Once again, she was pretty beat up by the opponents in the tournament. It was nothing new, however. Just an annoyance. A day at the beach with teammates Jen Lalor and Jessica Fischer and Steve Slain riding bikes, taking naps and baking in the sun did wonders. And she knew it would. She was beginning to understand her body more and more. She didn't, however, always pay attention to it.

> *April 24, 1995:*
>
> *There was a great service at church. The service was on praying — when and how to do it. Joel Hunter, our minister, was saying that God is not a "tooth fairy God," meaning you don't put your problems under the pillow and expect Him to take them away. That's exactly what I do. I have to understand that God is giving me nothing I can't handle, and He gives me the means to get through it. He will bless me with something better (something a thousand times better than I can imagine if only I stay faithful). Just because He doesn't take my problems from me right now, it doesn't mean He's not listening. I can't give up. I have to keep praying and be thankful.*

MICHELLE'S FAITH IN GOD WAS GROWING. HOWEVER, IT WAS not easy. An extremely strong-willed person, Michelle had always relied on herself, and no one else, to accomplish her goals. Great athletes learn to do that. When a player realizes they are the game-breaker or the game-maker, they strive to take control of the match. A truly great player is one who can win it by themselves, a player who wants the ball — demands the ball — when a goal is needed. Michelle is that kind of player. She is also that kind of person. When trying, and often struggling, to promote women's soccer around the world, Michelle knew that if she didn't take the initiative, it might not get done. It was her job, she thought, and no one else's for the simple reason that she was in the best position to do it.

"Due to the way I communicate and the passion of my beliefs and desires for myself, my team, and women's soccer, I don't put up with much," says Michelle. "It frustrates me to no end when people play games for power. And because of the strength and intensity of my feelings about the people these decisions and actions are affecting, I often cannot keep my mouth shut. Inevitably, that puts me in hot water with the powers that be. They don't, I believe, appreciate this player, this woman, disagreeing with them openly or privately about their policies and priorities. But I feel if I don't say anything, it will never be said. And if I don't do my best to change it, or at least express my opinion, then I won't forgive myself. It's an endless battle."

Michelle always had been the one behind the wheel. Even when she and Amy Allmann terrorized the UCF campus in a bike box, Michelle was the one in the front end of the box. In every situation, she depended on herself to get the job done. It didn't matter what the job was. If she deemed it important, she would press diligently to accomplish the goal. But now it was dawning on her that she would have to give up some control, delegate responsibility to God. It wasn't until later that she completely realized she had to hand over the keys and let Him drive.

ON APRIL 28, 1995, THE USA EMBARKED ON THE ROAD TO Sweden tour, a grueling six-game, coast-to-coast road trip that started in Georgia and ended on Canada's West Coast. This would be a true test of Michelle's health and determine the level of contribution she would be able to make in Sweden. She scored a goal in each of two wins over Finland, one in Decatur, Ga., and the other in Davidson, N.C. She was pleased with the way she was playing, but she had begun measuring her performance in goals scored and minutes played. "I got a goal and ninety minutes in the first game," she said. "And a goal and forty-five minutes in the second."

The U.S. Women's National Soccer Team was becoming more and more popular. The players were finally being recognized for their athleticism and skill, as well as for simply being nice people. Thousands were beginning to understand what hundreds knew previously. The increased publicity was welcomed by the players, and they handled it very well. Practice sessions were open to whoever showed up, and after each game the players usually stayed long enough to sign autographs for anyone who wanted one. Michelle saw years of hard work paying off, but she couldn't help wonder if the publicity came too late for her. In 1991, when Michelle was so dominant, hardly anyone knew the USA had won a world title. Now, the younger players on the team were the ones the cameras were seeking. But Michelle was still reaping the rewards for her years of hard work.

THE USA BREEZED DOWN THE REST OF THE "ROAD TO Sweden." The team beat Brazil twice and Canada twice. Michelle scored four times in limited action, deciding to take herself out of each of the last four games. "Before the World Cup, there was a lot of concern about my health," she says. "I thought I'd never make it. I had played my first ninety-minute game in two years just five months prior to the World Cup. So I was fairly nervous about the level I would be at in June. Would I be able to compete? Would I be able to help my team win? Would I be able to play like Michelle Akers? Although those questions entered my mind frequently, I never voiced them to anyone except Steve Slain, my best friend and our strength coach/massage therapist. He refused to hear any of it. He said he knew I would be there, and he had complete faith in me. Many times, he was the only one who really believed it. And I have no idea to this day why he thought that."

May 19, 1995:

We slaughtered Canada 9-1, and the team played very well, especially Gumby (Carin Gabarra) and Lil (Kristine Lilly). I got two goals, both off PKs. Took myself out at the half because I was feeling sluggish and EBVish. Bummer, but reality. I didn't want to make a mistake and not be able to recover for World Cup. During autographs, I signed a girl's forehead. Her mom probably killed her when she got home.

AS THE WORLD CUP INCHED CLOSER, MICHELLE WAS AGONIZING over her condition. Could she play like the Michelle Akers of 1991? Would she have enough energy? The CFIDS was still jumping up and announcing itself on a regular basis, and Michelle was worried. The week before the team left for Sweden, Michelle did very little training. She was simply too tired from the cross-country journey and the seven-games-in-five-weeks schedule.

May 30, 1995:

I don't know how I'll get through the World Cup. All I can do is pray. God will take me through it in the way He wants. I hope it's a fun WORLD CUP and not a terrible struggle. I'm sick of fighting uphill. I am terrified and excited about it at the same time. I suppose these are the same feelings I had before '91. It will be tough to put the same game plan into effect this time — try to make the moment less important in my mind, play for fun, let go and focus on the game. So many distractions. Keep praying.

Chapter Thirteen

THE U.S. WOMEN'S NATIONAL SOCCER TEAM ARRIVED in Sweden on June 1 to defend their world title. The 1995 FIFA Women's World Championships would not start for another five days, and Michelle was full of enthusiasm and nervous energy. She could not wait to get started. Throughout her career, waiting for games to begin was always the hardest time for Michelle. Once the whistle blew, it was a huge relief. She could just play soccer. In Sweden, the waiting was even worse. She was anxious about the competition, and she was a little nervous about how she would perform. Not only did the USA have a title to defend, but Michelle felt an obligation to live up to her billing as the best women's soccer player in the world. She couldn't wait for the whistle to blow.

Michelle's friend and confidant, Steve Slain, did not make the trip, however, staying behind to have back surgery. Michelle missed him, and so did the team. She talked to him frequently by phone, and they traded encouragement. To compound the wait, the team was a bit stir-crazy, and they killed time by playing practical jokes on each other. Unbeknownst to Michelle, Amanda Cromwell, her roommate, stole Michelle's playbook and hid it in another room. Michelle thought she'd lost it. Facing the team-imposed fine for losing your playbook, Michelle frantically tore the room apart searching for it. Amanda finally produced it. Michelle accused Amanda of breaking the "roommate pact" and retaliated by putting her shower shoes under Amanda's pillow with a note attached that said, "Get a whiff of these, sucker!"

On June 4, parents of the team members arrived, and they were a welcomed sight for Michelle. Having her family, her support group and fan club around her eased the tension. But it also reminded her of the standards she wanted to live up to. She knew what her family was expecting to see on the field. She believed they wanted to see the Michelle of 1991, so dominant, so strong. Michelle wanted the same. Her teammates looked to her as well. They did not count solely on her, but they knew life would be easier if the old Michelle took the field. "Knowing Michelle as a person and as a player, I always expect great things from her, just as she does from herself," says teammate Carla Overbeck. "With Mia playing as well as she was playing, and Carin and Michelle, we had high expectations."

June 1, 1995:

The team looks and feels ready. There's a quiet confidence. Less giddiness than in '91, more experience and calmness now. I'll just have to wait to see what comes up. So far, it flashes between victory – sinking to my knees in relief and happiness, running crazy around the field, hugging everyone, crying. Or walking off the field with that awful feeling in the pit of my stomach, wanting to punch each player on the other team as they are celebrating what we wanted so badly. I wonder what will happen.

Foudy brought her diary from '91, and it was great to go back. Hers was very inspiring. We should read what she wrote after the final party – hilarious, but very moving. Funny how each one of us believed so passionately that we would win. Fouds thinks this is the key.

THROUGHOUT HER ENTIRE CAREER, THE TYPE OF SOCCER shoe Michelle wore was of utmost importance. Her shoes at the World Cup in Sweden were very important and a source of major controversy. Her feet, shorter and wider than most female players, required added support on the outside. If the shoe was too narrow, Michelle would spend most of her time re-tying them, looking for adequate support. Michelle's shoe of choice was adidas. The company's trademark three stripes down the side actually served to provide added support to the outside of her foot. But since she was sponsored by Umbro, she was required to wear either Umbro shoes or Nike shoes, because Nike was the official sponsor and outfitter of the U.S. National Teams. Both Nike and Umbro made attempts to design a shoe that would give Michelle the support her feet needed. Both efforts fell short. While she was with Umbro, Michelle was allowed to wear adidas Copas, as long as the brand name and other identifying marks were blacked-out. Previously, while she worked Post-to-Post soccer camps, which she and her ex-husband Roby owned, Michelle discovered another shoe that was comfortable and provided necessary support. Reebok was the sponsor of Post-to-Post, and they sent shoes for all the staff members and clinicians to wear. One day, Michelle picked up a pair of Reebok Integrity shoes and liked the way they felt. Oddly enough, after that Michelle was allowed to wear non-blacked-out Reeboks in training and in games. So leading up to the World Cup, Michelle wore either blacked-out adidas shoes, or non-blacked-out Reeboks during training sessions, and there was no comment from any of the United States Soccer Federation hierarchy or from Nike. At that time, there seemed to be no concern as to what shoe Michelle would be wearing in the World Cup. But there was, and it came at the absolute worst time imaginable.

On June 2 in Sweden — four days before the first World Cup match — Michelle wore Reebok shoes in practice, like she had the previous four days. Now, however, there was a problem. "The situation began to get heated," Michelle recalls. "The USSF told me there is a problem with my shoes, and our administrator, Pam Perkins, asked me if I had adidas Copas with me. I told her I did, but they were brand new and would need some time to be broken in. I was aware of the increased tension, but I continued to wear the Reeboks." On June 4 — two days before the first game — Michelle met with a representative from Nike in a hotel in Gavle, Sweden. She was told that she would be allowed to wear blacked-out adidas shoes. She explained again that her adidas shoes were not broken in and she would prefer to wear blacked-out Reeboks. What's the difference, she reasoned, blacked-out is blacked-out. The next day, Michelle and Nike met again, and she was told that if she wore anything but Nike — no blacked-out adidas, no blacked-out Reeboks — she would have to be prepared for the consequences. Michelle took this to mean that if she did not wear Nikes, she would not play. By phone from the United States, team general manager Tom King confirmed the same edict to Pam Perkins, who informed Michelle. Michelle was stunned. She had tried Nikes, but without the support in the sides, her foot would roll and slide to the outside when she changed directions sharply, creating a tendency to roll her ankles. She also got blisters on both big toes and her feet cramped up. When she wore the Nikes, they stretched, and she had to continuously re-tie them. Michelle was getting annoyed and frustrated. Why couldn't she just wear the shoes in which she was most comfortable?

On June 6, Michelle went to Sandy Bodecker, head of International Soccer for Nike, to plead her case one last time. Two hours before the match was scheduled to start, Sandy and Michelle came to an agreement on the shoes. She would wear blacked-out Reeboks and she would try to wear Nike shoes in the 1996 U.S. Cup, and she would hear a proposal from Nike on future endorsements. With precious time and energy spent fighting over whether or not she could wear the shoe in which she performed best, Michelle took the field in blacked-out Reeboks.

The whole mess with the shoes just added to Michelle's stress level. But finally, the World Cup had arrived. Now she could just play, duplicate her 1991 performance and help her team to the championship platform again.

Chapter Fourteen

MICHELLE NEVER GOT THE CHANCE TO DO ANYTHING in the World Cup. She didn't get to show the world her talents again. She didn't get to thrill her family and friends. She didn't have the opportunity to walk to the podium as a world champion again. Six minutes into the USA's first game, Michelle dropped back into her own penalty box to help defend a Chinese corner kick. One of the USA's strongest headers, Michelle took two steps backward and jumped to head away the corner kick. From behind her back, a Chinese player flew toward her. The Chinese player, not seeing Michelle's backpedal and thinking she had a clear shot at the ball, snapped her upper-body forward to gain power on her header. Michelle headed the ball first, knocking it out of her opponent's path. The Chinese player, with all the force she could muster, banged her forehead against the back of Michelle's head. Michelle was knocked unconscious immediately. She crumpled to the ground in a heap, twisting her right knee as she landed.

Michelle's teammates had seen this scene thousands of times. Every game, at least once a game, Michelle crumbled to the field in pain. She was usually the victim of an under-skilled hack, whose only hope of stopping Michelle Akers was cutting her legs out from under her. Other times, against more skilled opponents, she was simply on the receiving end of countless hard and clean, but nonetheless painful, tackles. "Usually Michelle gets whacked to the ground and then bounces right up," says Tiffeny Milbrett, who watched from the bench as Michelle laid on the ground. "But this time, she didn't even move. I was worried for her, saying to myself, 'C'mon Mich, get up!' And then horror set in when I realized I was the one who would go in for her. Then I heard Tony say, 'Milbrett, warm up!'" After several minutes of being tended to on the field, Michelle waived off the stretcher and walked to the bench with the help of the medical staff. The head injury was something that would keep her out of this game, and possibly the next. But the knee was more serious. Was that it? Six minutes? After four years of struggling, hours of training ... six lousy minutes? Unbelievable! Michelle was devastated. She so looked forward to the World Cup, and here she was injured before she could break a sweat. The most important thing right now, she thought, was to help the team win any way she could. She had to be strong and not sulk about sitting on the sidelines. She had to be supportive, not disruptive, and she amazed herself with the way she was able to behave.

"I was remarkably calm," Michelle says. "Miraculously calm, to be more accurate. It was God's doing, not mine. I remember getting slammed in the head and waking up on the field thinking, 'Whoa, what the heck just happened?' The team was around me telling me to stay down, and I could tell it was serious. Then the trainer and Doc came out, and I remember waving off the stretcher. That was about the end of my memory for a couple days."

Michelle and Tiffeny Milbrett leave the field in Sweden.

Photo by Mike Stahlschmidt

Ironically, Amy Allmann, Michelle's friend from college and former teammate on the national team, was in the broadcast booth doing color commentary for ESPN2. "It was my job to describe the replays," explains Amy. "When they showed the replay of her injury, it was the first time I'd seen it. I couldn't say a word. There was dead silence. My broadcast partner, J.P. Dellacamera, finally had to tap me on the shoulder and tell me to say something. Everybody who was watching was probably thinking, 'I wonder how the U.S. is going to play without her.' I was thinking, 'I hope she's not paralyzed.'"

Amanda Cromwell, Michelle's roommate in Sweden, had never seen anything like it, and it scared her. When Michelle left the hospital and went back to the hotel, she slept for twenty-four straight hours. "I was devastated for her," says Amanda. "I was bringing food into her and trying to help her. But she was just out of it. I'd never experienced anything like that before." The next day, when Michelle was finally able to get up and around, Amanda, Doc Brown and Michelle went for a walk. "We felt it would be good for her to get some fresh air, so we went for a twenty-minute walk," Amanda says. "We ran into someone Michelle knew from the time she spent playing in Sweden, and they had a short conversation. From the way they were talking, Michelle definitely knew this guy. Later that day, I asked her who he was, and she said, 'What guy? What're you talking about?' Then I realized that she didn't remember the guy, the conversation or the entire walk."

June 9, 1995:

So it's two games into the World Cup and I have played only six minutes. Doc Garrett says I got over the Epstein Barr only to get the Shanghai Shaft. Funny. Yeah, real funny. I got a mild concussion along with an MCL sprain. I had to go to the hospital for a CT scan (yes, I have a brain), and poor Dad was there again with Dr. Garrett. He was scared to death for me. I swear I will send him to an early grave. Anyway, head-wise I'm okay, but the knee is painful. Doc Brown says to push through the pain for a quicker rehab. Our motto is "Good pain is hard to find." Appropriate. I'm running already (straight) with lots of grunting and swearing. I'm not as broken up about it as expected. This EBV experience has made me so dang tough. I called home to pick up my messages and everyone was really worried about me. In the whole scheme of things, missing this World Cup is a disappointment, but not the end of the world.

TIFFENY MILBRETT REPLACED MICHELLE IN THE LINEUP in the first game and scored a goal to help the U.S. build a 3-1 lead that they would eventually surrender in a 3-3 tie with the Chinese. Milbrett, playing in her first major international tournament, was nervous and a bit frightened. But she gained strength from Michelle.

"Her injury scared the heck out of all of us," Tiffeny says. "Personally, I was very scared. Because of her injury, I was playing far sooner than I or anyone expected. And with that, Michelle helped me a lot more than she knew. Probably the one thing Michelle gave me was that she was just always the same Michelle to me. And in my times of fear of being in the World Cup as a rookie, it helped just knowing that however I played, whatever I did, she would always be consistent with me. She would help me when I needed it. I would ask, she would tell, just as anytime before. Being able to trust in her made me want her to get back playing as soon as she could. Her being the same old Michelle to me, even in her time of crisis, meant so much more to me than any piece of information or bit of advice. All I can remember is that through her pain and her hell, she displayed complete strength. Support for the team seemed to be her first concern. She really never seemed to show any emotions about it, but I'm sure she spent many times alone, frustrated and crying.

"Just being in Sweden was the result of a long comeback for her," continues Tiffeny. "She had battled CFIDS and numerous injuries, and Sweden was to be her rebirth from all the setbacks.

To have her go down as seriously and as quickly as she did, was like getting a huge blow to the ribs. It knocked the wind out of the entire team. But that was nothing compared to what it did to Michelle. I think all the hope, confidence and spirit she built up from that long, long road back, came crashing down just as she did when she received that concussion."

Michelle woke up the day after the injury in a haze from medication and the concussion. When she awoke, she found little messages and stuffed animals around her hospital bed and on top of her. Various teammates and friends had written her notes of encouragement and also expressed their feelings of admiration and inspiration for her. "I was overwhelmed," Michelle remembers. "I told April Heinrichs, one of our assistant coaches, about it. I was wondering why I never knew this before and why they had never told me. April offered this: 'Maybe it takes someone to be knocked down, or weak before others feel like they can respond or tell them how they really feel.' Interesting. I learned that people open up through weakness, not through strength. I had been so strong for so long, but the way to really make an impact on people was to let them share in my struggle. I'll never forget that. You have to be very strong to show weakness, and people connect with that.

"Then in the locker room before the first game after the injury, something happened that I'll never forget. I was struggling to remain composed for the team. I didn't want to be a distraction. I wanted to contribute, so I felt it was important that they saw me as okay, that I was taking it all in stride. We had taken to writing "Steve Slain" on our sock tape. He couldn't come because of back surgery, so we were playing in honor of him. I walked in the locker room and they all had 'Mich', or '#10', or 'Mufasa' on their socks. Then in the pre-game huddle, Carla said, 'If you get tired out there or feel like giving up, I want you to look at the bench and see Michelle. She never gives up, and we won't either. Let's play for each other from this moment forward.' I almost lost it again.

"The team helped me accept the consequences of the injury and the new role I would have on the team," Michelle continues.

*Michelle's teammates wrote her name
on their sock tape when she could not play.*

Photo by Mary Harvey

"The hard part was facing my family and convincing them I was okay with it. It was so sad seeing my Dad and my stepmom. They were so disappointed and sad for me, and it hurt to see them like that. It crushed me, in fact. I just wanted everything to be okay for their sake. I was thinking, 'Now this! What else am I going to put them through?'"

June 10, 1995:

I struggled at first with my new role on the bench. It's tough being on the sideline. Doc said I was handling it like a "champion." Good thing I had sunglasses on because I almost cried. People think I have it all under control, but it's very close to the surface. At any moment, I feel like I'll lose it. God, give me the strength and grace to get through this one. So far, so good.

DESPITE THE AGONIZING CIRCUMSTANCES OF HER INJURY, Michelle was having fun with her team. And, as usual, she was the victim of practical jokes. "She's pretty gullible so I always use that to my advantage," says Kristine Lilly. Mary Harvey remembers the moment caught on home video that the team finds hilarious. The teams at the World Cup had to travel from one venue to another by train, and one such trip was an eight-hour journey for the Americans. At a stopover halfway through the trip, Michelle was standing on the platform in the train station with her bag. Led by Lilly, three team members asked her to hold their bags as well so Michelle now stood holding four bags. Soon, other teammates began to hang their bags on her. "When you watch the video, there's Michelle with about thirty bags hanging off her," says Harvey. "She had one hanging off her forehead. It was hilarious. She looked like a coat tree."

*Michelle, the coat tree,
in Sweden*

Michelle was in good enough spirits to joke with Amy Allmann during a televised interview before one of the games. "I had to do the pre-game interviews with the players," remembers Amy. "I hated that part of the job because everybody was talking in my ear, and I couldn't concentrate. I had to interview Michelle, and I asked her a really stupid question, something like, 'What do you remember from the collision?' She said, 'Amy, I was knocked out. I don't remember anything.' So we had a good laugh about that. Then they showed the replay of her injury, and I asked Michelle to describe it. It was the first time she had seen it. As they showed the replay, Michelle said, 'I went up for a header ... here comes the Chinese girl, and ... Ouch! That must have hurt.'"

TRYING TO MAKE EVERYTHING RIGHT AGAIN, MICHELLE rehabbed her knee furiously. Without her, the team had one win and a tie in its first two games. After the 3-3 tie with China, the USA beat Denmark 2-0. It looked to be a safe bet the team would advance to the second round, and Michelle wanted to re-enter the tournament at that point. So she huffed and grunted and swore her way through workouts, pushing through the pain as Doc Brown had advised — good pain is hard to find. If it was at all possible for her to make it back for the quarterfinals, semifinals or finals, she would do it. If the team could beat Australia in their final first-round match, they would win their group and be one of two teams from their group to advance to the second round. But they would have to score more goals against the Aussies than China would score against Denmark in a game that was played simultaneously at a different venue. The U.S. would have to do it without Michelle.

June 11, 1995:

We beat the Aussies yesterday, 4-1. Crazy game. We were getting the scores from China-Denmark, and as China kept scoring, we had to keep scoring to ensure our number-one spot in the group. Plus, the fact we were down 1-0 with thirty minutes left didn't help much. It was exciting and gut-wrenching. Fouls came

off the bench to score first (header), then Beef (Joy
Fawcett) scored on a toe-poke in a scramble, then
Carla on a PK, and finally, Debbie Keller (it seemed
to take forever to go in) in the last minutes to put
us in first place. Tony kept yelling, "Okay, one more
goal!" Then China would score another, and Tony would
yell, "We need one more!!" I thought we'd never be
able to do it.

AFTER THE AUSTRALIA WIN, THE USA ADVANCED AS THE
winner of its group. On June 13, the Americans would play Japan
in the quarterfinals. Michelle told herself she was ready. She
would play if the team needed her, but it turned out the Japanese
were no match for the Americans. Kristine Lilly, who Michelle was
calling the "best player in the tournament," scored two goals —
blasting a free kick from 35 yards that completely confused the
Japanese goalkeeper. Michelle and Kristine spent hours of practice time perfecting those kicks. "That was our time to hang out
and talk or whatever," says Kristine. "When I first started working
on them, I would try to take them just like she did, because it obviously worked. Then she told me to do whatever worked for me and
not to try to copy someone else. That helped me a lot. When I scored
the one against Japan, I ran over to the bench looking for her." Lilly
launched another rocket from the top of the penalty area, and the
score was 3-0 at halftime. There was no need for Michelle to enter
the game. Her fragile knee would be saved for the semifinals.

June 14, 1995:
    The press is really hounding me. After every train-
ing session, they surround me. "Will you play? How's
the head? How's your knee? I saw you only kicking
with your left foot?" ... Aaaaargh. I'm getting more
press than the people who are playing.

AS THE PRESS BOMBARDED MICHELLE WITH QUESTIONS,
she gracefully fended them off with thoughtful, yet vague answers.

The U.S. would play Norway in the semifinals, and the last thing the Americans wanted to do was give the Norwegians their lineup and game plan. Away from the field, Michelle had questions of her own. For the first time since she tried out for her college soccer team, she had doubts.

June 15, 1995:

I start tonight, and for the first time ever I'm terrified to play. I don't know what I will be able to do. My knee is sore from only thirty minutes of light training yesterday. What will it be like after an intense forty-five? Tony said he doesn't expect me to "fly in and rescue the team," but I think a lot of people do. I just want to make a small difference. Actually, that's a lie. I want to make a huge difference. I want to score goals, be a threat, be the best player out on that field. And it's killing me knowing I won't be that player.

MICHELLE COULDN'T WAIT TO GO HOME. IT HAD BEEN A tough tournament, a tough week, month, year for her. The tough-guy routine was wearing thin. It was more exhausting than actually playing, she said. And to top it off, she had twelve family members to convince. "Dad is dying for me," she said. "Every time I see him, he seems like he's trying to will me to be better, to be okay with what's happened to me. He's worse than I am, on the verge of crying, trying to be brave for me. Poor Papa, I know his heart is breaking for me. It will be nice to be home, anonymous, doing what I want, not pushing the envelope for a while. Only four more days. "

"We were just pretty sad for her," says her dad. "I was trying to figure out what was going on with her, what she was really dealing with. I think a lot of things just came to a head at the World Cup. There was her illness, her age and her divorce. But the tournament would just last a week or so. I was trying to figure out

Michelle had a lot on her mind
prior to the semifinal game of the 1995 World Cup.

Photo by Mary Harvey

what was next for her. Any parent at any level doesn't want to see their child suffer. You never get used to seeing your kids get hurt. It's just a basic parental instinct to protect your children."

MICHELLE'S INSTINCTS WERE CORRECT. SHE PLAYED THE full ninety minutes and the U.S. lost 1-0. Norway scored early, and the USA valiantly tried to tie it for the rest of the afternoon, pounding shots at the Norwegian goal. Michelle, limping most of the second half and playing one-footed because of her gimpy right knee, could not make the difference she'd hoped to make.

The Americans took the loss very, very hard, and Michelle was devastated. For her, the World Cup that never really started ended much too soon. "We came out flat," she explained. "Others have explained it as either nervous, tentative or scared. Whatever it was, it was not the U.S. team I know. I did okay. I did my best, but on that day it just wasn't enough. My thoughts immediately after the final whistle were to not cry, to not show the everyone how much it hurt. I just wanted to get to my family. It was awful to shake the Norwegians' hands, to talk to the press, answer the obvious, the stupid, and the humbling questions. 'Yes, the Norwegians were better than us today. Yes, they deserved the game.' I had to stand there as the world watched us come up short, knowing that I would be seeing those images for the rest of my life. Is it better to lose and know you didn't play your best, or lose and know you just didn't have the talent? Tony and I both knew I was going to struggle in the game, but he chose experience over youth. And to this day, I don't know if we were right in that decision. But you can't second-guess that now. You never know. If I had gotten one chance, the game might have been different. So I played the game one-legged, limping all over that dang field. I had no business being out there, but again, I refused to give up. I did the best I could ... and my team lost."

There were a lot of tears on the field that day. Several U.S. players sat with their heads in their hands, or laid on the field covering their eyes. The disappointment of not successfully defending their world title was too much for some to bear. Michelle was determined not to cry, though, and she made it through some tough stretches. "Jen Lalor broke my heart," Michelle remembers. "She came over to me and said I was 'such a stud,' that I was an inspiration and she felt so bad for me. This team is so selfless, always more concerned with the struggles of others. Thorny (Thori Staples) was the same way. She said she'd give me her leg if she could. Tony almost made me cry in the pre-game. Same stuff — I was an inspiration, very courageous. Honestly, anyone else on the team would do the same. I still can't see what the big deal is."

The tough guy act vanished as Michelle was finally able to leave the field. She headed to the stands, the section where her parents were seated. It was a long walk, that fifty yards. "It was hard not to cry," she says now. "And I lost it when I got to my family. For some reason, I was the only player to go over there, and when they noticed I was coming over, the whole U.S. contingency started cheering. I couldn't look at them. I kept my head down and when I saw my Dad, I hugged him and cried. He cried too. Everyone was crying — Sue, my brother, Eva. It was sad, and it was very intense. It was more than just a lost soccer match. I felt like my family and I had gone through so much and fought so hard, but we wound up short. After a few minutes, I walked away from them and had to deal with the press, who immediately made mincemeat out of me, my performance and my team's performance. I had to choke back the anger to remain professional and be a respectable loser. By this time, of course, my team was long gone and waiting for me on the bus."

The Americans went on to win the third-place game, beating China 2-0 on goals by Tisha Venturini and Mia Hamm. Michelle was back on the bench, wishing it was all over and she was home again. All she wanted to do was relax, hide and forget about it all.

June 18, 1995:

The final between Norway and Germany was horrendous, and the banquet was even worse. It seemed each day was meant to rub our face in the disappointment of losing. The Norwegians won every award and came in to the banquet singing. Gumby and I had to give our '91 awards to the winners, both Norwegians. Gum came back to the table crying. Tony said some good stuff on the bus ride home – Never forget the feeling we have this night. The margin of victory on the field is so small, but the margin off the field is huge. The Norwegians were in the limelight, receiving awards, holding the trophy; the U.S. in the back of the room, unnoticed, and forgotten. Hopefully, that message will stick with everyone and will propel us to the winners' platform in the Olympics. We now look toward the Olympics. This team will be ready. I will be ready.

ON JUNE 21, 1995, MICHELLE WAS BACK IN ORLANDO. SHE was up at 5:00 a.m., sipping coffee, listening to Cheryl Crow on her new headphones and writing in her journal. But nearly a week after a loss that occurred halfway around the world, she still could not bring herself to write about the experience in Sweden. It remained too painful. Well-wishers were calling, and most of the callers wanted to know the same thing — "What happened?" But they had to leave messages. Michelle was not taking calls. As soon as she knew the answers, she'd tell them. For now, however, all she wanted to do was rest. It would be another two weeks before she wrote her Sweden conclusion in her journal.

November 1996

1991 vs. Canada

Photo by Jon Van Woerden

1991 vs. Canada

Photo by Jon Van Woerden

**1991 FIFA Women's World Championship
Final vs. Norway**

Photo by Phil Stephens

1995 FIFA Women's World Championships in Sweden

Photo by Mike Stahlschmidt

1996 Olympic semifinal vs. Norway
Photo by Brett Whitesell

August 1, 1996, Athens, Ga.

Photo by Perry McIntyre

The Gold Medalists.

Front row: (left to right) Mary Harvey, Brandi Chastain, Briana Scurry, Carla Overbeck, Carin Gabarra, Joy Fawcett, Tiffeny Milbrett. **Back Row:** Tiffany Roberts, Cindy Parlow, Staci Wilson, Shannon MacMillan, Mia Hamm, Michelle Akers, Julie Foudy, Kristine Lilly, Tisha Venturini.

Photo by Phil Stephens

Chapter Fifteen

July 5, 1995:

I WENT HOME FROM SWEDEN AND WAS UPSET FOR WEEKS. But I worked through it, began rehabbing the knee, got checked and okayed by a neurologist, and got on with my life. I went back to church and began to understand the purpose, or part of the purpose, of my World Cup experience. I soon realized it was a blessing and an incredible witness to the strength and trustworthiness of Christ. I started to see my life — my disappointments, as well as the victories — in a new light. I have struggled to put into words the testimony or praise of what God has done with my life the past three or four years. I kept thinking, "Who cares about this stuff? Who really wants to know?" But I kept getting this little nudge to write it down, so here it goes.

Having CFIDS has been the most frustrating, depressing experience of my life. By far, this is the toughest thing I have ever fought. The recovery process is long and tedious and requires positive thinking and the utmost patience, which is not a strong trait for me. There were days I wanted to die or just give up because of the headaches, fatigue and fever. Recently, I've learned CFIDS has been a blessing. Being so sick made me rethink my life, and as a consequence, I filed for divorce last September and started going back to church at the Northland

Community Church in Orlando. Slowly, ever so slowly, I began to make a comeback in my health and soccer. Now I am happy, at peace, and following this crazy call on my life.

It's been tough, the last year and more. I feel like I am constantly being thrown huge challenges. I overcome one and another is thrown in, seemingly from out of nowhere. At times, I am tired of having to overcome. I want it to be easy for a change. I want things to run smoothly. But as I look back at how far I've come, I realize God has blessed me and is still blessing me. I am the kind of person that sometimes has to, literally, be knocked down or hit over the head to get a point across. So through these hard times — CFIDS, injuries, divorce — God has forced me to open my eyes, to look at my life, to find the "narrow road" again. To listen, love, and follow Him. To trust. I now know how my successes and struggles in soccer are to be used. I know the frustrating, disappointing, tough experiences are for a reason. It's all to prepare me to do something on down the line, to give me an experience to share, to test and strengthen my faith and trust in Jesus.

So that brings us to where I am right now. I heard our preacher, Joel Hunter, give a sermon last weekend, and I'm excited to start in earnest. I swear he looks right at me sometimes when he talks. His message to me was "Forget about what others think. Forget about the logistics of how or why. Put your eyes on God. Listen and learn. Trust. Just go out and do it."

Here I go.

Chapter Sixteen

T HE FIRST PART OF MICHELLE'S JOURNEY INVOLVED introspection. She needed to interpret what had happened in Sweden and determine what good came out of it. She thought of 1991. She thought of 1995. She thought of her struggles and the commitments she made in order to play in both tournaments. One tournament was exhilarating; the other devastating. Why?

"Defining Moments," she decided. "I've heard the phrase before, and it has left a lasting impression on me. As I drove home one day, I discovered that struggles and defeat — not triumph — create an intimate bond between people. It's amazing to me that a situation which brings you to your knees, something that causes you to feel immense pain — whether emotional, physical, or spiritual — is the overriding link between each of us. In my perspective, when people describe triumph in and of itself, it's shallow and meaningless ... unless there has been some insurmountable mountain that had to be courageously climbed in order to achieve their goal or dream. Otherwise, I can't be excited for them. Why should I? They haven't really been tested. Defining moments for me come in the form of the struggle to achieve. The struggle to overcome. It's the struggle that makes you triumphant. It's not necessarily the medal around your neck that makes you a champion.

"Winning the World Championship in 1991 was a defining moment for me," Michelle continues. "I struggled, we struggled, to overcome all obstacles — lack of support, money and experience. We struggled to win. We wound up with the trophy, but the mountain we climbed to get there was long and grueling, rich with sacrifice and hardship. In that World Cup, I discovered what I was capable of. I had the talent to be the best in the world. Winning that World Championship did not come easy, but I was rewarded for my efforts with a first-place title. That moment for me on the podium was a fantasy, a fairy tale that does not often come true. We all lived happily ever after. It was the 1995 World Cup that truly showed me who I was. I found victory despite defeat. And defeat, disappointment, heartache and frustration, are more real in this world than the fairy tale ending of 1991. The key is to shine in all circumstances, to experience Christ's victory instead of our own failure or defeat."

SO MICHELLE STARTED TO SORT THROUGH HER LIFE, prioritizing everything. The defeat in Sweden had made her stronger and a whole lot wiser. She learned she had gone too far, and God slowed her down. With a quick flick of a Chinese player's head, God reminded Michelle that it was only soccer. No big deal. It's just a game.

Michelle had never considered herself a "religious" person. In fact, she doesn't consider herself religious to this day. To Michelle, religion seems very stuffy and impersonal. Christ to her, however, is very personal and extremely powerful — very real. Her 1995 World Cup experience forced her to look at her relationship with Christ in a new light. And soon, Michelle came to realize that soccer was not all that important. She had lived for soccer for so long. It was the center of her life, and for her to come to the realization that there were more important things in life than soccer amazed even her. The most important thing in her life now was to do what God wanted her to do and become who He wanted her to become. His plan for her had become much more rewarding and exciting than any plan she could have come up with herself, and she became willing to sacrifice everything in order to achieve God's purpose for her. She learned nothing else really mattered except her relationship with Him. She learned to trust Him to the point of, yes, even living without soccer. And she soon found it remarkable that this realization enabled her to enjoy soccer even more.

"This was the start of trusting my life to God," Michelle explains. "I say the beginning because before this, I didn't fully, completely give Him everything. I was still hanging on to soccer —

for me, not for Him. And there were a multitude of other things I still had for myself. It took the sequence of events in that World Cup to begin to trust Him. I found myself out of the World Cup after so much sacrifice and pain. Yet, He got me through that terrible time — despite and because of that horrible experience — and blessed me in many ways. He enabled me to handle all of it with grace, strength and maturity. Once I came home, I was a mess. But by that time it was okay to be a mess. It didn't matter by then. I didn't have my team to worry about."

Back in Orlando, Michelle had yet another knee surgery, her eleventh. After the surgery, she spent most of her time in the weight room working her way into top physical condition again. She was, however, paying very close attention to what her body was telling her. When she needed a rest, she took it, but still agonized over it.

January 10, 1996:

I was once what you call a low-maintenance person, no special attention or needs. Independent and strong. But now I need all these special considerations, excuses and rules to live by. I am high-maintenance. I'm fragile. For example, to play for the national team is tough. Sometimes I can practice and sometimes I can't. I'm not very reliable. I hate getting sympathy for feeling awful and yet, I want people to understand how bad I feel, and that I'm not just copping out. I want to train. I just don't have the gas to get the job done and still be able to function later on in the day. I dread having to tell Tony I can't practice. And the thing is, I can practice. But if I do, I'll be awful. Then the next day I'll feel even worse. So technically, I can, but I won't. I hate that.

"FOR THE FIRST TIME IN HER LIFE, MICHELLE HAD LIMITED resources," says Colleen Hacker, the team psychologist leading up to and during the Olympics. "She had always wanted it all, could do it all, and she did it all. She never had to make a cost-benefit analysis. Now on a daily, hourly and sometimes minute-by-minute basis, she had to weigh all these factors — opportunity versus responsibility, go to the grocery store or be able to make it through the entire practice. She constantly had to measure the cost of the activity. For most of us, these are separate. For her, what used to be thirty quick choices became heavily laden decisions. What impressed me perhaps the most was that she handled it all in a very quiet, humble, gentle way. No one's attention had to be diverted to her. She didn't require any sympathy from her teammates. Chronic Fatigue Syndrome is certainly not an illness that lends itself to consistency, and she went through an almost minute-by-minute uncertainty and concern. But she faced it all with a calm, almost warrior-like spirit. A lot of people would bemoan the fact that they weren't able to join the team for a meeting or a dinner or an outing. But she wasn't denying herself fitness. She gave up the fun things, and she protected the hard work."

AFTER MICHELLE SUCCESSFULLY REHABILITATED HER knee injury, she jumped back into action. The national team had put together a nineteen-game schedule leading up to the Olympics, and in the third game of the slate — Michelle's first since rehabilitating the knee — the Americans faced Norway in Tampa, Fla. In the first five minutes, Michelle injured her right knee again, but she stayed in the game. Two days, later, the team played Norway again, this time in Jacksonville. While warming up for the game, the knee did not feel right so Michelle had the team doctor take a look at it. His news was devastating. "He said, my medial collateral ligament was fried, and that I needed reconstructive surgery right away," says Michelle.

The knee would take four to six months to rehabilitate, and the Olympics were five months and seventeen days away. That was it, she thought. No Olympics. Michelle left the locker room in tears and bolted to the nearest pay phone to call Eva Ferara, her friend and business manager. Fans were still entering the stadium, and they stopped Michelle to ask for autographs. After she spoke to

Eva, Michelle settled down a bit and tried to accept her fate. But as she attempted to re-enter the stadium, the ticket-takers would not let her back in. So there she stood, crying, in full uniform, her Olympic dream shattered, arguing with security to be allowed back into the stadium. Finally, she hopped a fence and re-joined the team on the bench.

The next day, Michelle went to Doctor Jim Barnett, who was more familiar with her knee history. "It's ripped and pretty bad," he told her. "But you can rehabilitate it." She went back to work.

Much of Michelle's time before the Olympics was spent rehabbing and working on fitness.

Photo by Perry McIntyre

Chapter Seventeen

MICHELLE NO LONGER TRIED TO BE ALL THINGS TO all people. She was focused on her next goal — Olympic Gold!

"I realized just as I had to adapt my person to this illness, I had to adapt Michelle the soccer player to CFIDS," she says. "I could no longer be the fittest, strongest and quickest all the time. I had to choose my moments. But I prayed for those moments to be there when I needed them. If the CFIDS was running its course that day or week, I couldn't think straight, I was slow and fatigued, I had nothing to offer my team except maybe my presence. Was that enough? In the meantime, when I was healthy, I could change the kind of player I was and conserve the explosiveness and energy for the days and games to come. I could be smart, savvy, skillful. Let the ball do the work, as they say. I could be a veteran and orchestrate the game. Take it over mentally. But could I do that?"

As Michelle adjusted her game, the team was making some adjustments as well. While they all truly expected Michelle to be on the field when the Olympics began, they weren't sure which Michelle would show up. Would it be the tireless Michelle Akers of old, chasing down loose balls, making forty-yard sprints to open spaces or dribbling toward the opponent's goal carrying defenders on her back. Or would it be the technically smart, savvy veteran initiating plays from the midfield, cracking shots when the opportunities came and winning air duels on corner kicks and in midfield,

"Unlike in the World Cup, we were prepared for what might happen," explains Kristine Lilly. "We could make adjustments if we needed to cover for her at certain times. For example, we'd give her more passes to her feet instead of making her run for everything. Before she was sick, I used to send her running to the corner every time I got the ball. That was all I knew how to do — look up the line and pass it to the corner. I would say, 'Michelle, I'm so sorry. I'm making you sprint every time.' But she was like a machine, and every time I sent her to the corner, she'd get the ball. After I improved, I could find her in the middle more."

The team that represented the USA in the Olympics was a much more seasoned and intelligent squad than the ones which played in the 1991 and 1995 World Cups. "I remember before 1991, Carin, Michelle and April, our three forwards, were warming up before practice," says Lauren Gregg, the team's assistant coach since 1989. "They were standing about ten yards apart whacking the ball at each other. I mean they were drilling it at each other. I asked them what they were doing, and they said, 'We're getting ready for the types of passes we'll be getting.'" Since '91, the team had become much more skilled, but in the 1995 World Cup, they still played a bit out of control at times. From the World Cup to the Olympics, the main emphasis was on keeping possession of the ball with intelligent, easy-to-handle passes. And since the Olympics would be played in the July heat of the Southeastern United States, the U.S. coaches wanted to be sure there was no unnecessary running. In short, they wanted to be smarter.

"Michelle had to learn to adjust her game," says Lauren. "And the team had to learn, too. When she was younger, Michelle played the same way all the time — with reckless abandon. She could find the ball anywhere in any environment. But she made all the adjustments she needed to make."

Michelle's teammates made their adjustments fairly quickly. They learned not to depend on her as much as they had in the past. They still expected great things of her, just as they did every member of the team. But when the Olympics rolled around, they would be prepared to play with whichever Michelle Akers took the field. They would be prepared to win.

The CFIDS had Michelle back on the roller-coaster. When it was bad, it was really bad. When the bouts were over, she felt rejuvenated and fresh. But she was determined not to fall into the same trap, by over-doing it when she felt strong. She knew too well that pushing CFIDS too far would keep her out of action for too long. Her training time had become a precious commodity, and she did not want to waste it. "All her decisions revolved around rest," says Julie Foudy. "That was her number-one priority. Her concern was always her performance, and that's amazing to me — so unselfish. It's so ironic that she has this disease ... I mean of all people."

On April 18, Michelle arrived at the national team's training camp in San Diego. The team was preparing for the Olympics, and Michelle was busy trying to sort out what kind of soccer player she was going to be. It was not an easy task. "With this illness, her very identity was called into question," says Colleen Hacker. "She questioned her value and her contribution. But she was ready for whatever player showed up that day, whichever Michelle came to the field — clear thinking and confident, or kind of stunned, confused and exhausted. She knew how to adjust."

In preparation for the Olympics, Michelle struggled with her health, and trying to determine what kind of player she could be.
Photo by Doug Menuez

April 15, 1996:

Each day, I have to assess who will show up. I have to figure out how to compete and play as an impact player. I have to figure out what kind of work I'll be able to do. Do I bust or save? Quick-thinking or a bit slow tactically? Strong or weak? Can I take defenders on one-on-one, or is it just dishing off today? And how do I prepare myself in warm-up? Conserve? Do I tell Tony or not? And then there's my mental preparation. What is my role today – healthy, or sick? And when my role changes because I cannot fulfill who I want to be based on my energy and mental capabilities, I have to be able to make the transition to the next Michelle Akers. It has to be done positively, quickly and effectively. And then I have to accept the disappointment of not being who I want to be. So who is it today?

And to deal with all this stuff alone! To battle back session after session, day after day, is so very tiring. Yesterday, I cried in the shower, exhausted and at the end of myself. Lord, I can't make it through this day. Please give me the strength because I just cannot do it.

SHE GOT THROUGH THE FIRST SESSION. EVEN HAD A GOOD day, she said. And three days later, she was trumpeting her return. "Phew! I'm Back! I am Back!" she said. "Semi, anyway. We played Holland, and I lasted the full ninety minutes ... barely. I scored a goal on a header and played okay." She was not the Michelle Akers of old, but she felt she was getting there. Progress was made, and she had fun.

April 18, 1996:

I'm enjoying the team socially, and I'm enjoying my walk with the Lord and my Bible Study Fellowship. I'm enjoying the sunrises and sunsets here in San Diego. Things are just tough for the moment because of the anxiety of being healthy for the Olympics. I just want to be able to compete — without reservation. The thought of having to conserve or play within a limitation scares the heck out of me. Can I be satisfied with that level and still play soccer? I don't know.

Steve keeps saying I make such a difference when I am on the field (I'm Cal Ripken, yeah right). But what he doesn't know is the incredible effort it takes just to be out there. Each game and practice, I have to take this deep breath to gather the energy and focus to compete. Will there be enough left in the tank for that extra something it takes to be the best? I'm fearful I'm using all I have just to be out there. What a journey.

MICHELLE HAD A NEW SPONSOR. SHE SIGNED WITH REEBOK after the World Cup and started helping Reebok develop and promote a new line of women's soccer shoes and apparel.

"I think everything came together very fortuitously for both Michelle and Reebok at about the same time," says Peter Moore, senior vice-president of Reebok's Global Soccer/Rugby Division. "She had a long-standing and mutually beneficial relationship with Umbro. From my perspective, Umbro could have done a little more with her from a marketing standpoint. But Umbro is not a huge company in relation to a Reebok or a Nike. At a time when Michelle's Umbro relationship was coming to a close, we were really working hard on a strategy to develop women's soccer because our heritage as a brand has always been the woman athlete. We had been watching her with concern over her illness, and to be honest, there was the feeling that she was past her best, and even damaged goods. But we didn't hesitate in our negotiations. First of all, women's soccer wouldn't be anywhere close to what it is today on a world-wide basis without Michelle Akers. Secondly, when we look at her as an individual, she typifies everything we felt we needed to stand for as a brand — her determination, the way she carries herself as an athlete and as a woman, and her ability to conquer what for most mortals is a completely debilitating illness. Most people with Chronic Fatigue can barely get out of bed and go to work, never mind play a sport at a world-class level. As we were coming to closure with our agreement with her, I met with Michelle when she was just coming off a three-hour workout. The people who were with me had never met her before, and her determination to conquer this illness and play soccer at a world-class level was an inspiration to us all. At that point, not only did we put her as our premier soccer icon for women, she actually became a key part of our Olympic TV spots with Emmitt Smith."

When Michelle signed, Reebok already had Julie Foudy in the fold. Peter Moore and the people at Reebok approached Julie before they pursued Michelle. "Julie was the first player we picked up," says Moore. "And looking back, Julie was the first woman soccer player to do a commercial. We did a TV spot where we found old footage of her brother bouncing the ball off her head. We spent several million dollars primarily with Julie showing women's soccer as a vehicle for women's sports. We sat down with Julie, and not wanting to offend her, explained that we felt Michelle was the premier player from the perspective of pure women's soccer marketing. Julie, on the other hand, is a great role model that happens to play soccer. If she wasn't playing soccer, she'd be doing something else at a world-class level. She will be part of our women's sport shoe campaign, and Michelle will be part of our women's soccer campaign. Julie actually encouraged us to go after Michelle. There were no egos involved, and that was very enlightening to us all. They are good friends and have been through a lot together. With many athletes, there would have been a lot of jealousy, but Julie encouraged us to bring in Michelle. Once we knew that Julie was comfortable, we went after Michelle, and we're thrilled it has all worked out."

Michelle had promised herself she would cut down on her off-field activities. She would do only what she had to do in order to play in the Olympics. However, Reebok wanted her to make a television commercial with Dallas Cowboys running back Emmitt Smith. Michelle felt she had missed enough practice time with her illness, and she was concerned that taking time to shoot a commercial would be too much. The shoot was scheduled for Dallas on April 21, one day after the U.S. would play Holland in Fullerton, Calif. On April 24, the team had a game against France in St. Louis. On the 28th, they were scheduled to play France again, this time in Indianapolis. Michelle felt it would be just too much, and she wasn't sure if it would cause problems within the team if it appeared she was working on her own timetable. So Michelle turned down the commercial, telling Reebok that she could not make it.

Michelle's friend and business manager, Eva Ferara, completely understood, but she also saw this as a chance of a lifetime for Michelle. Eva sent Michelle a fax that read, "As a friend and a person who has been with you through this illness, I understand where you are coming from for the team, and I understand your need for rest. But after talking to Peter Moore, my business side is prevailing my thoughts. Reebok is setting up camp for a week to shoot all of the ads that will run on NBC for their Olympic buy. Your commercial with Emmitt is a key part. It will cost Reebok a significant amount of money if they cannot shoot your segment. Peter said it would be cheaper for them to charter a jet to fly you in, which they will do if they have to. Mich, they really need you on Sunday, April 21. I honestly feel the visibility for women's soccer that this commercial will generate should be reason enough for the team not to get upset. If you will have a change of heart, I will personally fly in and take care of everything so all you would have to do is follow my lead. I will wake you when you are needed. I really think from the business side, this is big!"

Michelle did not want to do the shoot for the commercial because it was not something for the team. It was just not a good enough excuse, she thought. After Reebok agreed that this would be the last time before the Olympics her presence would be requested, she finally agreed. She and Eva flew to Dallas and Michelle made a commercial telling Emmitt Smith that if he wanted to play in the Olympics, he needed to play the "Real Football." After the filming was completed, the camera crew told Eva what a welcomed relief it was to work with such a willing athlete. And in the three games surrounding the shoot, Michelle scored in each game.

"We all felt that was our best spot," says Peter Moore. "Not only was it Michelle's first network TV commercial, but it showed a sense of humor. It also positioned women's soccer and Michelle Akers against one of the premier athletes in the world."

Chapter Eighteen

I N EARLY 1996, WHEN MICHELLE WAS AT THE NATIONAL
team training camp in San Diego, she saw Hillary Johnson on
Good Morning America discussing a book she had written
about CFIDS, titled "Osler's Web." Michelle, thinking "Osler's Web"
was the definitive book about her illness, picked it up and enthu-
siastically started reading. Like almost all CFIDS sufferers who
read the book, Michelle was shocked and depressed. Johnson presented a gloomy picture of the illness and offered almost no hope.
Michelle, who read the book to learn more about the disease,
found it dim and depressing. Fortunately, she decided to dig deeper and found that the American Association for Chronic Fatigue
Syndrome (AACFS) disputed many of Johnson's claims.

In an official response to Osler's Web, the AACFS wrote,
"Although Ms. Johnson is a keen observer, she has not been
trained in the key disciplines required to interpret the events she
is describing," the statement begins. "The Board of Directors of
the AACFS therefore re-emphasizes a point that we make repeat-
edly to the medical community and patient groups: the most
reliable information on any illness can only be obtained through
peer-review literature, which involves repeated testing of ideas
and the application of results to a wide variety of circumstances.
Therefore we caution the reader about the accuracy of Ms.
Johnson's conclusions."

The AACFS went on to say it was "no surprise that an author
will use information to make the points that will convert the reader to his/her interpretation of the facts. However, it is critical that
the reader recognize that Ms. Johnson is able to say whatever she
wishes without the same type of critical review that goes into sci-
entific publications."

In retrospect, it was not a good time for Michelle to be reading Osler's Web. Her hopes of a recovery began to look extremely dismal.

April 20, 1996:

I am in San Diego for national team camp. We play the Dutch tonight, and I'm struggling again with this stupid virus. Whatever it is — a virus, cancer, who knows. I've been reading Osler's Web and the more I learn, the more powerless I seem to be against this giant mystery disease.

MICHELLE BECAME MORE AND MORE FEARFUL OF HER ILLNESS and the effects of it on her career. She soon determined that she might not be able to play in the Olympics. Soccer, it seemed, was out. There was too much at risk. She was ready to give in to the illness. "I was really, really struggling to keep up mentally and physically, although no one would probably guess," Michelle remembers. "I had become good at hiding it. 'Osler's Web' was scaring the bejeebers out of me, and I knew I couldn't keep up the charade of trying to be healthy enough to play for much longer. My body just wasn't able to keep up with the demands of travel and training day-in and day-out. I was getting worse. As far as keeping up a strong front for the team, I was reaching the end. I was sick and exhausted in all aspects of my life."

No one, except for Steve Slain, Michelle's father, stepmother and Amanda Cromwell, knew everything Michelle was going through. The information she gave the coaches and staff was very factual — nothing about feelings or fears. She decided long ago to keep all that away from the team. Fortunately, Michelle had a great deal of resources at her disposal, many more than the typical CFIDS sufferer. "The book scared and enlightened me to the point of giving up my personal and isolated fight. It forced me to ask for outside help," Michelle says. "The author took a very negative slant and made a few rather large unsubstantiated and biased comments about CFIDS. She is not generally accepted as the spokesperson for CFIDS, and she presented one side to a very confusing and ambiguous illness. But I was glad I read the book because it made me realize I needed help. However, if I was a 'normal' person, the fear factor from reading the book might not have been beneficial. Most people don't have the contacts and resources I do. And consequently, they cannot dissuade the fear and ignorance of the illness and enlist support to overcome CFIDS. Most people have to fight it alone in utter confusion and frustration."

Michelle found outside help from Dr. Paul Cheney.

> *April 28, 1996:*
> *Thank God, Dr. Cheney is now part of the equation. Let's see what he can add to my artillery to fight off this illness. I am also starting to understand how often I will have to deal with disappointment — in myself.*

Chapter Nineteen

COLLEEN HACKER GAVE MICHELLE A BIT OF ADVICE THAT helped her continue moving in a positive direction. "God can't guide your steps unless you're taking some," she told Michelle. So Michelle took more steps. As a last ditch effort, she sent an email to Dr. Cheney. Paul Cheney was one of the first doctors to fight for and investigate CFIDS. He branched off with his partner, Dr. Dan Peterson, from the original CFS clinic in Incline Village, Nev., to start his own — The Cheney Clinic in Charlotte, N.C. World-renowned and a bit controversial in his treatments, Dr. Cheney's name was prominent in "Osler's Web." And he represented Michelle's last hope. To Michelle's complete shock, Dr. Cheney responded to her email the next day. "It was absolutely unbelievable that I got an appointment with him because people have to wait months to get in, and I got a hold of him in a matter of days," she says. Michelle called to set up a phone consultation for the following week. The result of her initial conversation with Dr. Cheney was that she had two choices — quit soccer or try the Elimination Diet.

Dr. Cheney's treatment program lasted ten weeks, and the day Michelle was scheduled to conclude her treatment was July 21, 1996 — the day of the first game of the Olympic soccer tournament. Another gift from God, Michelle thought. On the advice of Dr. Cheney, Michelle started the Elimination Diet. She felt results in one week. She took supplements — multi-vitamins, antioxidants, B Complex, ENADA, which contains NADH, Magnesium, CoQ10. She also began juicing pounds and pounds of carrots a day and mixing the carrot juice with UltraClear.

May 19, 1996:

As of now, I am on a new diet recommended by Dr Cheney — no gluten, sugar, caffeine (yeah, right!), dairy, alcohol. It is tough, but one week into it, I felt a huge improvement. Amazing.

THE NEW DIET GAVE MICHELLE SOME HOPE, AND HOPE was all she needed to keep fighting. She fully understood that diet alone was not the answer to her illness, but she was encouraged by the early results. She was also beginning to feel stronger spiritually and could clearly see the direction in which she was headed. "I'm happy and at peace," Michelle said. "I am learning to really give God my life for the first time. I have learned to look at life like an adventure. It's something we have to go after. We have to take risks and live, rather than stand still or run away. I read in a book that when Jesus came into contact with people, they were changed — whether they wanted to be or not. I want to be like that. I want God to change people through my presence, my actions, my words, my choices and by my life."

Chapter Twenty

DESPITE MICHELLE'S APPREHENSIONS ABOUT THE player she would have to become, she was playing pretty well, certainly making a difference. From February to the end of April, the U.S. played ten games and Michelle played in all but one, scoring four goals. The team was playing well, gaining confidence in a new ball-control style with every match. Included in the ten games were a win over Norway and two wins each over Sweden, Germany and France. The only setback was a 2-1 loss to Norway, but the Americans came back to beat their rivals 3-2 two days later.

On May, 12, the team played its first game in the 1996 U.S. Women's Cup, a three-game tournament with Canada, Japan and China played in three U.S. cities. Michelle and Tony DiCicco would still watch her playing time and monitor her condition closely. In the first game of the U.S. Cup, Michelle played well in a 6-0 win over Canada. In the next game, a 4-0 victory over Japan, she again made a difference. The USA and China both won each of their first two games and met in the final at Washington D.C.'s RFK Stadium in front of 6,081 fans. Michelle pounced on a loose ball thirty yards from the goal and drilled a shot to the corner late in the match giving the U.S. a 1-0 victory. Michelle was named MVP of the tournament.

May 20, 1996:

The USSF brought Pops and Sue in to see the China game in D.C., and I played well. I got the winning goal on a cracker of a shot. What a boost. It was a nice day. I felt like I had a small taste of what winning the Olympics will be like — so much relief, pride and justification that it was all worth it. Finally something positive has come of this mess.

111

ON MAY, 11, 1996, MICHELLE PROVIDED A STATEMENT TO Congress on CFIDS Awareness Day. She was invited to give the speech in person, but was too sick to attend. In attendance that day was Dr. Peter Rowe of Johns Hopkins University. A day later, Dr. Rowe sent an email to Michelle and then followed up with a phone call to her at the team hotel in D.C. He invited Michelle to Johns Hopkins Hospital to take the Tilt Table Test to possibly diagnose her as having Neurally Mediated Hypotension.

An upright tilt table test is prescribed for people who have a history of something called "recurrent syncope" or passing out. The test is performed to discover if a patient exhibits one particular cause for passing out. The cause is termed neurally mediated syncope. The condition is caused by an imbalance of the nerves that normally control your heart and blood pressure. In individuals with neurally mediated hypotension, there is a miscommunication between the heart and the brain. Just when the heart needs to beat faster — to pump blood to the brain and prevent fainting — the brain sends out the message that the heart rate should be slowed down. In response, individuals feel lightheaded or may faint because not enough blood is getting to the brain. If a person is diagnosed with neurally mediated syncope, it can usually be treated with medication and other medical measures that can decrease the over-reaction of the nerves and prevent the episodes of passing out from continuing.

The test is performed by strapping the patient to a special table called a tilt table. The patient lays down on the table and a heart monitor, blood pressure cuff, and an oxygen saturation measuring device is hooked up. The doctor adjusts the degree of tilt to an almost standing position, then gives the patient an adrenaline-like medication to increase the heart rate and simulate exercise while standing still.

Some researchers have claimed that CFIDS is caused by NMH. However, many physicians who specialize in the treatment of CFIDS believe that this blood-pressure regulation is simply another body system knocked out of kilter by CFIDS. So a day after her encouraging performance in the U.S. Cup, Michelle went to Johns

Hopkins for the Tilt Table test. If she was diagnosed as having NMH, it could supply some answers to the CFIDS, and possibly, some treatment and hope.

She was diagnosed as symptomatic for NMH, a huge, huge break in her treatment and recovery.

May 26, 1996:

I'm at two weeks on the Elimination Diet now and still feeling good. Unfortunately, part of the diet is taking a million pounds of supplements, which in most cases, would be fine, but one of the supplements has a drug banned by the International Olympic Committee. — D-Mannitol — and we have a urine test in two days. I am in trouble ... and for more than just this. Dr. Rowe volunteered the Tilt Table Test three days before the drug test. Part of the test is to inject the person with Isuprel which is a major stimulant and also a banned drug. So I am potentially in trouble for two banned substances. (Team doctor) Dr. Mark Adams and I declared both drugs and have written letters to the USOC, but we don't know how they will handle it if I test positive. If it isn't one thing ...

The Tilt Table Test was good and bad. Good, in that it diagnosed a problem (NMH) and bad because it makes you feel awful. I was shaking, weak, panting for air, sweating, dizzy, crying. It was awful. It took me a week to recover from it. The test showed I was symptomatic for NMH, but not conclusive because I didn't have the huge drop in blood pressure and heart rate. I am on salt tabs for treatment and will explore other options (banned drugs) post-Olympics if this doesn't help.

WHEN MICHELLE GOT TESTED ON THE TILT TABLE FOR NMH, part of the test included an IV with a synthetic adrenaline — a substance banned by the International Olympic Committee.

She was so excited about a possible diagnosis, it slipped her mind to think of a diagnostic medical test being a problem. Then on the plane home, it hit her. She might be in trouble. Michelle immediately told team director Pam Perkins, then trainer Patty Marshak, then team doctor Mark Adams. They decided to confess up front what had happened. Michelle wrote a letter to the United States Olympic Committee, as did Dr. Rowe at Johns Hopkins. Mark Adams followed it up with a phone call to the head of drug testing with the USOC. The plan was for Michelle to take the drug test and be prepared for the worst. In the meantime, she stopped taking any supplements and hoped her body would get rid of everything in two short days. She drank gallons of water, coffee, and, of course, sweated in the Florida sun during practice.

May 23, fifty-eight days before the first Olympic game, was test day. Michelle brought in all her supplements, as requested, and found out that another one of the products — ENADA — had a banned substance. "I was furious," Michelle says. "I had called the USOC drug hotline twice when I started the supplements weeks earlier, and I was okayed to take them. We called again. They okayed it again. I called back yet again with tester present, and then the guy on the hotline says it was banned. I couldn't believe it. So now I had two possible banned substances in me. Great! We waited on pins and needles for two weeks. Tony, Pam, everyone was freaking ... I mean we were freaking out. We had gone through all this stuff and now, this! What else?"

But to Michelle's complete surprise, she tested negative.

Chapter Twenty-One

F INALLY, AFTER WHAT SEEMED AN ETERNITY, IT appeared Michelle had nothing left to overcome off the soccer field. The diet was working. She felt as good as she had in years. The team was together and getting along well. All that was left was to train for the Olympics and play in the matches as best she could. Finally, just soccer.

Her teammates were becoming more and more important to her. Some of the people closest to her — her father, Eva Ferara and Steve Slain — were all advising her to let people help. "I opened up and let others in," she says. "I learned to share myself, my struggle, my weaknesses, and rely on those that care about me. I let them help me and understand how hard it was for me at times. I was weaker, but in a way I was stronger. I became a stronger leader, a stronger influence, and at the same time, more vulnerable. Being vulnerable was a big, big step for me. My friends would probably say I began to 'feel' more or show more emotion, which actually scared the heck out of my close friends for a time."

So Michelle began to lean on her teammates a bit more. They were always willing to help, but Michelle didn't want to be a burden so she rarely asked for help. They had enough to worry about, she felt. She didn't want to distract them from their own preparation. Amanda Cromwell, who had overcome a serious knee injury to contend for a spot on the team in the months leading to the Olympics, was one Michelle let get close to her. They joked often about the day when Amanda was a high school senior and being recruited to play college soccer at Michelle's alma mater, the University of Central Florida. Michelle gave Amanda a call one day, and Amanda was awe struck. "Michelle Akers called me!"

she told anyone who would listen. Amanda couldn't believe it. But she went to the University of Virginia anyway.

"It was really hard to know Michelle," Amanda says. "She was just doing her thing. We always got along, but I wouldn't say we were close until just before the Olympics. She had her fun, joking around, playing practical jokes. But she was just Michelle the player. That was about it." During the months leading up to the Olympics, Michelle had days when she would have to leave practice early. Amanda would go to Michelle's house to check on her and often find her in bed, unable to get out. "You could tell just by looking at her that she needed help," says Amanda. "So I would go to the grocery store for her, or go get her a movie, cook for her, just take care of her. That's when she started letting people help her. She realized that if she asked, we would be glad to do whatever she needed. I think I was one of the ones she felt close to. It took a while for her to understand that people could help her and that it was all right to ask. I think she was surprised at how willing people were to help."

When Michelle left practice early, some assumed she was going to rehabilitate her variety of injuries. But most of her teammates comprehended the situation better than Michelle knew. And they understood she would do whatever it took to get on the field for the Olympics. Carla Overbeck was very aware of what was going through Michelle's mind. "Even if you miss a day of practice, you feel you missed out on so much," Carla says. "It's like you've been out of it for months. You know your team is out there training, and you feel like you're falling behind. And she's such a big part of this team. That's why we tried to keep her in the loop and let her know what was going on. We tried to let her know we understood that whatever she had to do to get better, that was what we wanted her to do. As a team, we knew she was struggling with this illness, and whatever she had to do to be one-hundred percent, we wanted her to do it. We had a lot of team functions that she couldn't attend, and we always called to check up on her and tell her what she missed. We kind of felt sorry for her. We knew in her heart she wanted to be there, but her brain and her body were telling her she couldn't do it because she wouldn't be able to train or she wouldn't be able to do her rehab. It was just understood that she was recovering from an illness, and this was how she had to do it. Everyone understood, absolutely."

Tiffeny Milbrett noticed some changes in Michelle as the Olympics neared. "It's always difficult to know exactly what's going on with Michelle," says Tiffeny. "She always seems so consistent, the same Michelle day-in and day-out. But as the Olympics neared I noticed her focus increased tremendously. It's hard to tell with her because she is always so focused and always doing what she needs to do to make her the best athlete she can be. But as the Olympics drew closer, I think she turned her focus even more inward, really withdrawing from everyone and doing what she needed to do to prepare completely and undividedly for one of the most important events of her life."

Cindy Parlow, one of the team's rookies, used Michelle as motivation. "To play with the illness is one thing, but to play at that level is amazing," says Cindy. "Her strength is incredible. It's completely motivating. I'd get up in the morning and say, 'Oh my God, I have another practice.' Then I'd see her out there busting, and I knew she was probably in a ton more pain than I could ever imagine. I would think, 'Forget my problems!' It's not just her, but the whole team in general. It's amazing the standards we set for ourselves every day in practice. Some days you think you are never going to reach that level, but you amaze yourself."

Michelle had become very good at doing exactly what she needed to do to get better ... and nothing else. As Carla Overbeck said, the team had complete trust that Michelle would make all the right choices. "Every decision effects you whether you realize it or not," says Michelle. "First, I decided what my priorities were for the long haul, and I could not waste a moment or ounce of energy. I was moving toward those goals and nothing else. I had to decide what was the most important thing for me to accomplish. During '96, my priorities were soccer and Christ. That was pretty much it. So I set my sights on the Olympics and what God wanted me to accomplish, and I went from there. Anything that helped me get healthy, fit or helped my soccer was a 'yes,' and anything that took me off the path of playing in the Olympics was a 'no.' So along the way, I weighed everything everyday on the basis of this principle. CFIDS people learn to do this so they can do the things they want to do. They save their energy for the activities that are important to them. The other stuff just becomes unimportant and even detrimental."

"THAT'S HOW SHE HAD TO THINK," SAYS CARLA OVERBECK. "She put her social life aside and did what was best for the team. That's a true teammate. As it got closer to the Olympics, we all wanted to do fun things, like go on Mac's (Shannon MacMillan) Waverunner, but you had to stop and really think about the consequences. If something happened to you, you'd be letting your teammates down. With her illness, she had to think like that for two years. She definitely put her team first, and getting herself ready to play was her number-one priority. It's too bad she couldn't just play. She always had to think about conserving energy. I've never been in that situation, so I don't know how it felt. It seems like it is a horrible way to do things. But she understood that."

When she felt strong enough to train, Michelle went at it full-speed ahead. Despite all the breaks she had to take, her body was still in the condition of an elite athlete. She made sure of that. Part of the national team's daily fitness regimen involves something called the "speed ladder." When players spread out across the field for sprints, they line up according to their speed — the slowest at one end, the fastest at the other. When a player beats the teammate on her right, they trade places so they are always racing the player closest to their own speed. "We are always really close on the speed ladder," says Kristine Lilly. "When she was battling back before the Olympics trying to get one-hundred percent, she would ask me to stay after practice and run four or five sprints with her so she could see where she stood. If she was two steps behind me, she'd say, 'Okay, I'll get you this time.' She has a really positive attitude in her training. She would never say, 'I'm so slow, I'll never get my speed back.' It was, 'Okay, now I'm two steps behind ... now I'm one step behind. I'll get you next time.'

"But," laughs Kristine, "she'll still never beat me."

THE NEW DIET WAS HELPING. MICHELLE'S BRAIN FOG WAS clearing up, and she was feeling as good as she had in five years. She started preparing her own food, cooking and packaging it for road trips, and the team's nutritionist would supply her with some.

The simple act of eating became a major production for Michelle. She couldn't touch ninety-five percent of what "normal" people digested through a typical day. But the price was well worth it. Feeling good, or decent, was the top priority, and the diet had proven itself to her. So she lived on gluten-free cereal, PowerBars, dried gluten-free soups, gluten-free bread, rice milk, popcorn, gluten-free pancake mix, corn or rice pastas, peanut butter and carrots ... a lot of carrots. When she needed it, her friends at a health food store in Lake Mary, Fla., would send her food on the road.

June 3, 1996:

This diet is still working wonders (thank you God). I have increased energy and stamina, balance, peripheral vision, strength. Wow! I am feeling better and stronger by the week.

WHENEVER MICHELLE ATE, HER TEAMMATES WERE instantly reminded of the price she was paying to play in the Olympics. "When she got on the gluten-free diet, she seemed to improve a lot," says Carla Overbeck. "It was funny. Food is such an important part of it all. It's your fuel. And she would get this stuff, and we'd all say, 'Let me try it!' Then we'd turn our noses up at it. It was nasty. I asked her, 'How do you eat that?' She said, 'If it's going to make me better, that's what I have to do.' She is such a true champion. She knew what she had to do to get better, and she stuck to that. And it worked."

But true to form, the rest of Michelle's journey to the Olympics was not an easy ride.

June 5, 1996:

Another day in the life ... Jeez. I hurt my stupid big toe. Can you believe that? I can't get one day's respite from controversy or injury. Nothing goes smoothly in my life. Can I just do something without complications? Just once? I was shooting. Jolly (Michelle Jolicoeur) blocked it and ouch! I played a little longer on it, but it hurt pretty bad. And as the day went on, it got worse. I'm going in today for X-rays. Now what?!

MICHELLE SUFFERED A GRADE-TWO SPRAIN OF THE JOINT that attaches the big toe to the foot. It swelled up like a balloon, she says. She couldn't put any weight on it, let alone run or kick a soccer ball. It was two weeks before she could put her shoe on. Like most every part of Michelle's body, the toe needed to be taped and she had to be aware of it when playing. But it was certainly not going to stop her. After living with a chronic illness, suffering numerous concussions, having eleven knee surgeries and surviving a drug test, she simply could not imagine herself announcing to the team that she was not going to be able to play in the Olympics because her big toe hurt.

The USA had two remaining tune-up games before the Olympic-opener on July 21 in Orlando. On July 4, the Americans beat Australia 2-1 in Tampa, and then defeated the Aussies by an identical score two days later in Pensacola. Tisha Venturini scored the game-winner in both games, and Michelle played well enough to give herself confidence heading into the home stretch.

July 7, 1996:

It's amazing how clear my mind is after being on this diet. And what's even scarier is how I've been functioning in a complete fog the past six years. Tunnel vision, I call it. It's scary. How did I ever survive without completely ruining my life? God can be the only answer. Thank God He was there showing me a glimpse of light to follow in this crazy path. I tried to play today with a migraine and decided to quit. No more of that unless I absolutely have to. No wonder I got injured so often. The team is looking good — fit, fast and focused. We are going to win. All the ingredients are there. I read my article in USA Today from '91 and discovered I feel exactly the same way for this one — confident, peaceful, prepared to win. I can imagine the feeling when we do it — awesome. A champion at last. Victorious, at last. Personally and professionally. What an exciting journey.

Chapter Twenty-Two

THE TEAM CHECKED INTO THE OLYMPIC VILLAGE IN Orlando, Fla., on July 18. The village was the University of Central Florida campus, Michelle's old college SWATing grounds. The team's practice field was the UCF soccer stadium. "The Olympics became a reality for me when we left our training center in Sanford, Fla., by police escort to the Olympic Village at the University of Central Florida," says Michelle. "Traffic parted like the Red Sea. And all of a sudden, we were somebody special — Olympic athletes. I remember thinking, 'Jeez, this is it! It's finally here!'" Michelle decided not to attend the Olympic Opening Ceremonies in Atlanta with the rest of her teammates. She was certain it would take too much out of her. So she stayed in the Village and rested. The chance of a lifetime, to march into the stadium with all the other Olympic athletes, was something she would have to do without. Again, she knew what she had to do, and she did it.

Early in the afternoon of July 21, a police motorcade arrived to escort the team bus to the Citrus Bowl. A helicopter circled the bus and checked the path ahead. By the end of the Olympics, the players will have developed friendships with motorcycle police, Federal Marshals, FBI agents and security personnel. Photo sessions with uniformed players and uniformed police officers with their arms around each others shoulders were common. T-shirts, balls, posters and programs were autographed regularly. The city of Orlando, an Olympic venue for soccer only, had adopted the U.S. women's soccer team as their own. And Michelle Akers became known as Michelle Akers of Lake Mary, Fla. "Everywhere we stayed, drove, or played, the security was outrageous," Michelle says. "Awesome, in fact. We had FBI, Highway Patrol, Riot Police,

Federal Marshalls, SWAT, Canine units — you name it, we had it. To and from the games, we were escorted by police with their sirens blasting. At practices, we had SWAT teams surrounding the field, helicopters flying overhead, guards at the exits and entrances, metal detectors, bomb dudes — all 'just in case.' The guys and gals on all these units were incredible! We never had a doubt about our safety. Besides, they were some of our biggest fans."

An hour and a half before game time, the U.S. players took a stroll across the field, checking out the turf and the stadium. They were mostly working off nervous energy. About eight thousand fans were in the stadium when the players took their stroll, making the cavernous Citrus Bowl look empty. The players had no idea what kind of attendance to expect, so they appeared thrilled with the small crowd. They waved to familiar faces with that "Look at me, I'm in the Olympics" kind of look. "We were thrilled," says Tisha Venturini "Hey, if we see a couple thousand people, we get stoked." When game time came, the players nervously walked from the dressing room to the tunnel that led to the field. Later, several players would call coming out of the tunnel one of their most memorable moments of the Olympics. Before the game, the locker room was filled with taping, headphones, food, water, bathroom breaks, stretching, prayers, and meetings. "Everyone has their own routine," Michelle remembers. "But eventually, we all wind up in the same place — the tunnel, waiting for game time. The tunnel is a special place for me. We stand together high-fiving, giving words of encouragement, and in general whooping and hollering about how awesome we are and what we are about to do to our opponent. The feeling between us in the tunnel was one of intensity and extreme confidence. We were ready, capable, and prepared to do this thing to the fullest. From the beginning, I absolutely believed we were going to win it all."

When the USA marched out for the opener, twenty-five thousand, three-hundred and three people screamed and cheered, waving flags, banners and signs. The eleven starters lined up next to the Denmark starters and strode out to the Olympic March theme music. "Once we were in the tunnel, and the music started playing, I was like, 'Oh my God! ... This is the Olympics!,'" says Mia Hamm. "'This is what I watched on TV growing up.' As I was walking out, I saw my family holding up their sign, and I saw my sister wipe her eyes. And then I started crying." Michelle, as she always does, searched for her family. "I have a routine when it comes to family and national team games," she explains. "As I walk onto the field, I search for my Dad, and when I find him we give each other — and whatever other family members are able to attend — the thumbs up and a wave prior to the National Anthem. It's truly special to have my family in the stadium. Often times, I have to choke back the tears because it means so much to all of us to be there together as a family. Pretty doggone cool."

Michelle described the pre-game ceremonies as, "In a word ... Awesome." Mia Hamm called it "electric." Publicly, Michelle would later say it gave her energy, but few would understand what she really meant. "What an experience," she says after reflection. "The crowds were absolutely tremendous in both numbers and sheer enthusiasm. Add to that the Olympic Theme and the National Anthem ... and whoa! Goose bumps and a major lump in the throat." The feeling the players had cannot be easily described. It has to be experienced. The players even struggle trying to explain it. Leading up to the Olympics, Tony DiCicco invited some former Olympians from other sports in to talk to the players, hoping to prepare the team as best he could for what they would experience. In a nutshell, the American players were told to think of their most emotional experience in athletics and multiply it by a thousand.

After the Olympic March ended and the players were lined up at midfield, came the announcement of "Let the Games Begin." All the emotion and the drama led to a concern for DiCicco. His players had worked so hard and trained so long for the Olympics, and now they were here. "It would have been very easy to be overwhelmed by the crowd," says Mia Hamm. The team, however, was focused. They were ready. But were they too pumped? The Americans had worked long and hard on composure, and they wanted to be a bit less frantic, more controlled, calmer. But here they were with twenty-five thousand, three hundred three people chanting USA! in a setting one thousand times more emotional than anything in which they had ever been involved. Now, still twitching and bouncing with adrenaline flowing through their bodies, the Americans had to calm down and play. "There was a concern," says Tony DiCicco. "I even tapered my pre-game speech, toned it down a little. It would have been so easy for them to get too pumped up. But we had a tremendous focus and were very confident."

MIA HAMM EXPLAINED THAT FOR THE FIRST TEN MINUTES of the game, she could not catch her breath. Julie Foudy said she had a good time making eye contact with fans in the crowd. Despite the distractions, the Americans were creating scoring opportunities. The only effect the excess adrenaline appeared to have on the players was it added about five feet in height to each of their shots in the first twenty minutes. Four chances sailed over top in the early going, but the USA was playing a near-flawless match. Denmark, apparently trying to expose weaknesses the USA showed in the 1995 Women's World Cup, overloaded the ball side defensively. The feeling was that the Americans were unable to change fields quickly enough to do any damage. That was old news. The U.S. deftly moved the ball and attacked down both flanks equally well. They were particularly dangerous on the left side, where Kristine Lilly was a constant threat. With ten minutes remaining before halftime — which would mean a desperately needed rest for the Danes — Tisha Venturini became the first American woman to score a goal in the Olympics. And it was gorgeous. With her back to the goal, Venturini let a Brandi Chastain throw-in bounce past her chest. She pivoted and knocked a perfectly placed right-footed shot to the far post from twenty yards out. The ball glanced off the keeper's hands, off the inside of the post and in the net. Less than five minutes later, after Michelle suggested she "pinch in," Mia Hamm sprinted on to Michelle's well-placed header and converted her breakaway to make it 2-0, effectively ending the hopes of the Danes. Tiffeny Milbrett would make the score 3-0 after a brilliant display of dribbling skills by Mia set up the goal.

After Milbrett's goal with forty-one minutes left, the U.S. worked the ball around patiently, driving the Danes crazy in the one-hundred-and-two degree heat. The USA's complete domination gave Tony DiCicco the opportunity he wanted. With twenty-eight minutes left to play, he subbed Michelle out of the game, and eighteen-year-old Cindy Parlow took her place. The crowd gave Michelle an extended standing ovation. The cheers were in thanks for all she had done for women's soccer. They were in honor of the strong game she played that day, and partially, in recognition that the game was now won. Only a few in the crowd, however, were cheering because they were aware of her struggle just to be on the field. Michelle spent her twenty-eight minute rest cheering from the sidelines, waving a towel to the crowd and having the time of her life. After the final whistle sounded, she and her teammates made a trek to every corner of the stadium, thanking the crowd for their support. They yelled to family and friends and waved to strangers. Michelle took her own sweet time. She donned an American flag and a Red, White and Blue hat given to her by a fan, and with a huge smile, she basked in the moment, making it last as long as possible.

As electrifying as it was for Michelle to come out of the tunnel, walking back in was like someone pulled the plug. While on the field for that first game — whether in the game or celebrating the win — Michelle was able to fight through the symptoms of CFIDS. The symptoms are notorious for exploding when the sufferer stops. Knowing this, Michelle kept going as long as possible. "If I can manage to keep moving or distract myself from my body, then I can keep going," she explains. "But, if I stop, it's like the illness catches up with me and I can't escape the repercussions. If I stop, I literally stop. And that's the end of that. I can ignore it for a while, and then it all just caves in on me. When the whistle blows and it's all over, I suck it up until I get to the locker room, and then I die. It's like I manage to hide it or keep it at arms length with all the strength I can muster, and then in the locker room, I can just be me. I can let my guard down and just feel lousy."

Before stopping, Michelle made it through the post-game press conference, where she told the international media that she was very pleased with the way her team played and that she simply "had a blast out there. " And then she collapsed in the locker room. But Dr. Mark Adams and Steve Slain were there to make sure Michelle immediately began preparations for Game Two. "At the end of each game, I would help her off and Mark would take over," says Steve Slain. "He'd hook up an IV bag and it really helped. Michelle would always have a migraine after games, and in general, she'd be a mess. The IVs were a medical necessity, and because of them she'd be okay the next day ... she could eat, anyway." After finishing her post-game medical treatment, Michelle would join the team on the bus back to the Olympic Village. "On the bus, she'd just sit there, looking awful, with about ten ice bags on her," says Foudy. "It was kind of funny. She was always piled under ice bags, sleeping."

The next day was very important to Michelle. This was her chance — her only chance — to rest and recover. As always, Michelle got up early, about 5:30 a.m. She went to the dorm kitchen and quietly made herself some coffee, the only part of the Elimination Diet on which she cheated. Then she would write in her journal or do Bible study, waiting for either Brandi Chastain or Steve Slain, also early-risers, to join her. They would watch ESPN and talk a bit before breakfast. After breakfast, Michelle would get a massage, stretch, and ice down her various aches, pains, bruises and pulls. "I went into the training room at the Olympic Village in Orlando," says Kristine Lilly. "And there's Michelle with an ice bag on her knee, ice bag on her ankle, ice bag on her thigh, her hand all taped, and hooked up to an IV. I took her picture. She just looked at me and we started laughing."

During the day, some of her teammates would head off to shop or look around, but Michelle would stay put. She would watch TV and take naps, all the while eating and drinking as much as she could to replenish her strength. After dinner, Michelle would hang

127

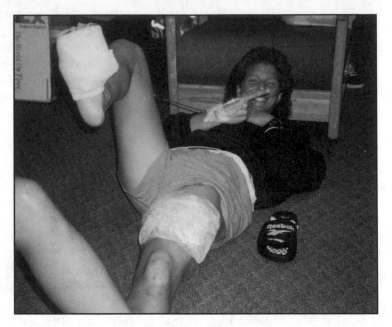

A common site in the training rooms at the Olympics was Michelle taped up, under ice bags, and hooked to an IV.

out with her teammates. They would watch TV and make fun of each other. Tisha Venturini, Michelle's roommate in the Orlando Olympic Village, knew exactly what Michelle had on her schedule. "She'd be in bed at 8:00 every night, just like a baby," Tisha laughs.

"We were there to win the Olympics, so my day revolved around what I needed to do to get my body and mind ready for the next game," Michelle explains. "Some people don't have to worry too much about that, but I had to be very conscious of every decision — large and small — because it affected my field performance so directly."

Day Three was the game with Sweden. The Swedes had lost to China in their first Olympic match two days earlier in Miami. The night after the Denmark game, Tony DiCicco was up late, and he was awake when the Swedish team arrived at the Olympic Village.

He talked to the team's coaches that night. They were very disappointed with their performance against China, and they told Tony, "We'll be better on Tuesday." DiCicco responded by saying, "That's what I'm afraid of." Sweden has one of the best professional women's leagues in the world, and the soccer-savvy Swedes are all skilled and experienced. But after losing to China, they were in a must-win situation. If they lost to the U.S., Sweden would surely be eliminated from medal contention. DiCicco's fear was having to face this team with its backs to the wall. "I had seen them in that position before," he says. "In the 1995 World Cup, they lost their opening game to Brazil. They were down 2-0 in their second game to Germany — this was elimination for them. But they came back and beat Germany 3-2. They play their best soccer when their backs are against the wall and they have to give it their all. We expected a combative, physical game." And that's just what the USA got.

The pre-game ceremonies were a repeat of the opener. A crowd of twenty-two thousand, seven hundred and thirty-four, pumped up the Americans. And fifty-eight seconds into the game, Tisha Venturini barely missed giving the USA an early lead, heading a Mia Hamm direct kick off the crossbar. Then the Swedes came right back with a near-miss of their own at the two-minute mark. With fourteen minutes and thirty seconds expired from the clock, Michelle sent a long cross to Hamm at the top of the Swedish penalty area. Mia popped a short cross to Tiffeny Milbrett, who headed it behind her to a crashing Venturini. Tisha drilled a diving header past the stunned Swedish keeper for the 1-0 lead and Tisha's second brilliant goal in two games. At the same time in Miami, China had taken a 2-0 lead over Denmark, emphasizing that no matter how well the USA was playing, China was performing at least as well.

At halftime, a quick rain fell, serving to increase the sauna-like conditions on the field, a situation that could only benefit the Americans. The hundred-degree heat on the field was certainly too much for the Swedish players. Michelle remembered a league match when she was playing professionally in Sweden when the temperature was in the seventies, and the players were taking extended water breaks. The U.S. players, having trained in the Florida heat for well over a year, were certainly accustomed to the conditions, and, in fact, thrived in the heat. The conditions, however, made it more difficult for Michelle. She would not completely notice, of course, until after the game when she collapsed in the locker room.

The Swedes battled the USA hard, grabbing arms, shirts, shorts, necks, anything they could to slow the quicker, faster Americans down. Eighteen times, Sweden was whistled for fouls, compared to eight fouls committed by the U.S. Mia Hamm was the main recipient of the abuse, being fouled five times ... officially. Many other apparent fouls went uncalled. Michelle was officially fouled three times, but she left the game with a variety of small injuries, including a charliehorse and a deep thigh bruise. In such a physical match, Michelle's ability to absorb punishment and still get the job done was crucial to the U.S. Still, Tony DiCicco wanted to give Michelle another rest and hoped his team would put the Swedes away early enough to give Michelle a jump on her recovery time. Then with sixteen minutes and thirty seconds remaining in the game, an uncalled foul against Mia Hamm turned in the USA's favor. Tiffany Roberts sent a pass to Hamm at the top right-hand corner of the Swedish penalty area. Hamm was pulled down by a Swedish defender, but the ball continued through to Shannon MacMillan. MacMillan, not waiting to see if the official would whistle the Swede for a foul, turned and fired the ball past the goalkeeper for a 2-0 lead. But with their backs to the wall, the Swedes scored two minutes later, and there was no chance for Michelle to rest.

"She was dying at the end," says Julie Foudy. "When she hit the wall, you could see it. It was so loud out there, you couldn't really talk to anybody. Because of my position on the field, I was one of the closest to her, so at every opportunity, I would get in her face so she had to hear me." In the final ten minutes of the match, Sweden, wilting in the heat, desperately tried for the tying goal. But urged on by the boisterous crowd, the Americans withstood the frantic pressure. Michelle pushed to the end, winning crucial battles in midfield and helping her team keep possession of the ball with thoughtful passes. "I was pleased with the way we played, but it was an indication of how difficult the competition would be," said Tony DiCicco.

After the game, Michelle and her teammates again celebrated on the field, soaking up the standing ovation and waving to the crowd. Several players grabbed a banner from the bench which read, "Thank You Orlando!" They showed it to every corner of the Citrus Bowl. In the locker room, Michelle went about her business of preparing for the next game. Some of her teammates would ask how she was feeling, and Michelle always responded with a quick and simple, "Good." Mary Harvey, the team's backup goalkeeper, noticed that Michelle seemed to be taking the attitude that if she said she was okay, she would believe it. "To me, she would just say, 'I'm fine.'" says Harvey. "That was the attitude. It made no sense to her not to be okay. She wouldn't let the people around her help her. I was asking because I cared. People care about her. It wasn't a burden."

The next day, after a light workout, the team took a chartered flight to Miami, where they would meet China for the final game of the first round.

WITH NINE MINUTES LEFT IN THE GAME WITH SWEDEN, MIA Hamm tangled with Swedish goalkeeper Annelie Nilsson during a goalmouth scramble. Mia twisted her ankle on the play and was carried off the field. X-rays after the game showed no break, but she would have to sit out the China game.

"We were a tired team at that point," says DiCicco. "This was our third game in five days, and the game against Sweden took a lot out of us. Conversely, Denmark went down to play China and tried to press China all over the field, and ... well, China was up 4-0 at the half and rested players. Their game was a lot different than ours. And finally, even though we were the seeded team, China played all their games in Miami. We had to travel. That didn't help us. Even if it's a short flight, packing up and moving a team is an all-day process. Going into the China game, both teams had qualified for the medal round. If I was looking for a good scenario, that was it — China wins both of their games, we win both of our games and we meet. It gives coaches the option to rest players. But because we were behind China in goal differential, I didn't think we could rest everyone we wanted to, and certainly we weren't going to risk Mia."

The absence of Hamm caused a lineup switch. Up front, Michelle would be teamed with Shannon MacMillan and Tiffeny Milbrett. The midfield was comprised of Julie Foudy and Tisha Venturini in the middle, Kristine Lilly on the left and Tiffany Roberts on the right. The back three remained the same — Carla Overbeck in the middle with Joy Fawcett and Brandi Chastain on the flanks. Bri Scurry was in goal. The weary Americans played an inspired match for the forty-three thousand, five-hundred and twenty-five fans. However, despite outshooting the Chinese 19-7, the USA could not find the net. The game ended in a 0-0 tie.

Tony DiCicco was able to rest a few players. Cindy Parlow and Carin Gabarra entered the match to rest Tiffeny Milbrett and Tisha Venturini. But Michelle lasted the entire ninety-minutes, her second straight full-game. "I liked what Michelle was able to do," explains DiCicco. "If she didn't think she could help the team, she would have taken herself out."

Despite all the precautions and preparations, Michelle was very tired at this point. And for the first time in the tournament, she felt she pushed herself too far. "My brother came down to the field and yelled at me to 'Dig deep!'" Michelle says. "He said I just looked at him — no animation or recognition whatsoever. I remember him doing it, though. I also recall looking at him and thinking, 'Jeez. I am giving it everything I have … there is nothing more. I'd better dig deeper. There's got to be more in there somewhere!' When I get empty like that, I kind of draw into myself. I try to find something inside and grab on to it so I can continue to play. It's like if I condense myself somehow and focus so keenly on the energy I do have, I can make it. I have learned to play within myself and do things on the basis of my energy level and on the cost of certain decisions. For instance, in a flash I can determine how much a certain play will cost me. Then I have to think, 'Can I afford to lose that amount of energy? Do we need me to do this or can someone else do it?' All these decisions come to mind, and if the answer is 'No, I cannot afford to do this and it is not the right time,' I play conservatively. If I am the only one who can make the play or if it is the time to risk it all, I go for it no matter what the consequences. If I drop, I drop."

After the game, she dropped. "She looked awful," says Overbeck. "She was sitting in the locker room in a heap. Every game, she gave every ounce of energy she had, and you could tell just by looking at her. I just can't imagine a human being going through that. We were concerned about her, but then we realized that she had been through this before. She knew what to do, and we understood that. We just let her do it. We had to help make sure she got all her things together and take her back into the training room. I can't imagine feeling that way. I was thinking, 'God, is it worth it?'"

Michelle's teammates, while concerned about her condition, thought it was better not to bring it up. "It was not really a topic of conversation," says Venturini. "We kind of knew what she was going through, but she's not the type to complain. We all just thought, "Well, Michelle is going to deal with it.""

Chapter Twenty-Three

THE TEAM LEFT FOR ATHENS, GA., THE SITE OF THE SEMI-finals and finals, directly from the Orange Bowl in Miami. Michelle's teammates watched a little of the men's game between Brazil and Nigeria, which was played immediately following their match. While the team watched the game, Michelle was flat on her back with an IV running into her arm. "The team left straight from the stadium to the airport," says Michelle. "It was a nightmare. The good news was we had a chartered jet so we got to stretch out. The bad news was I was sick as a dog. Plus, I had injured my knee in the game, so it was swelling up a storm. But I was too sick to care." The team flew to Atlanta, and Michelle checked into the Olympic Village in Atlanta, while the rest of the team went to Athens. The next morning, Michelle was up early, as usual. She grabbed a cup of coffee and went for gender-testing, as required by the International Olympic Committee. The rest of the team was tested when they went to the Opening Ceremonies in Atlanta, but because Michelle did not attend, she had to do it now. After a quick Q-Tip swab to the mouth, for gender testing, Michelle, completely wiped out, hopped in a car for the hour-long drive to Athens.

THE TIE WITH CHINA WAS REALLY NO BIG DEAL IN THE overall scheme of the tournament. Both teams advanced to the semifinals. But the USA would have to meet Norway, while the Chinese were faced with what was expected to be an easier challenge in Brazil.

Some of the players were secretly hoping to meet Norway in the finals. A significant part of the Olympic dream was seeing the faces of the Norwegians as they watched the Americans receive their gold medals. But that would have been an added bonus. The reality was that if the USA wanted the gold, they would have to beat the Norwegians at some point during the tournament. The semifinals would do nicely.

The team had an extra day's rest between the end of the first round and the start of the semifinal round — two days instead of one. Michelle certainly needed the additional twenty-four hours. "This was the beginning of the end," Michelle says. "I could barely shower, and I was just moping around wanting to die. My symptoms and weariness were more severe. My energy level on the field was diminishing earlier in each game, and the symptoms were lasting longer after each match. It was getting harder for me to play and recover from the CFIDS/NMH. The injuries were taking their toll as well.

However, there was no way Michelle was going to give up now. She had made it this far, and she was going to finish the tournament. And it became increasingly obvious as the tournament progressed that what she brought to the field was absolutely crucial to the U.S.

In addition to the usual symptoms, Michelle was completely beat up physically. Her right knee had to be drained the day before the Norway match, the result of a torn cartilage suffered in the China game. Her big toe joint was taped. Her hand was taped because of a sprained thumb and finger, and she had a pretty bad quad bruise from a charliehorse suffered in the Sweden game. She and trainer Patty Marshak joked that the entire U.S. Soccer Federation budget was spent to tape her up. "I didn't know how much was left in the tank," Michelle says. "So to say the least, I was concerned. I knew it was going to be a big effort on my part just to finish the game, let alone be an impact player. And I wanted very badly to play well."

For Michelle, the extra day's rest was not a luxury, it was a necessity. If she didn't have that day off, she says, she would not have been able to play. On the day after the China game, Michelle did practically nothing. She went to the practice field with the team, but she just stretched and watched her teammates jog around the field. The next day, she stretched and jogged lightly.

THE NEWSPAPERS WERE PREDICTING THE RECORD CROWD of sixty-five thousand that watched the USA play Norway in Guanzhou, China for the 1991 World title would be broken. But the crowd in Athens for the semifinals fell short of the record — eight-hundred and four people short. When the USA walked out of the tunnel, they discovered sixty-four thousand, one-hundred and ninety-six fans had paid anywhere from sixty to one-hundred forty dollars for a ticket to see them play. They all got their money's worth. Before the Olympics, the typical attendance for a U.S. women's game was about sixty thousand people shy of this crowd. "In Athens, we knew the fans were there for us," explains Julie Foudy. "In the tunnel, everyone was all excited. We were high-fiving everyone — each other, the volunteers, security, the FBI. It was great!" Michelle was as ready as she could possibly be at this point, and the crowd provided a much-needed boost. When she took the field, she was somehow able to again ignore her symptoms. However, she was very afraid she wouldn't be able to last for long.

Mia Hamm was back, but there still was a slight change in the lineup. DiCicco has a huge amount of respect for Norwegian midfielder Hege Riise, and he wanted a way to stop her. "Norway's men's coach actually nominated her for European (Male) Footballer of the Year," said DiCicco. "She is just a tremendous player." DiCicco knew exactly what to do. On his bench, he had one of his team's fastest players, who happened to be an extremely tenacious defender. Tiffany Roberts got the call to shadow Riise. Hamm and Milbrett would start up front, and the U.S. would play a five-man midfield for the first time in the tournament. Michelle and Tisha Venturini were in the middle with Roberts. Kristine Lilly would be on the left again, and Julie Foudy would make her first appearance as a right outside midfielder. The back was unchanged again — Overbeck, Fawcett and Chastain would play in front of goalkeeper Bri Scurry, who quickly became a favorite of the media when she vowed to "Run naked through the streets of Athens" if the U.S. won the gold medal.

Just as the crowd settled in to watch the match, Tiffany Milbrett woke them up with a long shot that Norwegian goalkeeper Bente Nordby had to backpedal to save. Forty-five seconds had elapsed from the stadium clock. There were two reasons Tony DiCicco wanted Michelle in the midfield — her distribution ability and her dominance on head balls. She started the game doing both very well. When the ball came to her feet, she dished it off quickly and accurately, starting moderately dangerous attacks. When the ball sailed anywhere near her in the air, she won the heading duels with the intimidation that amazed Anson Dorrance in 1991.

Tisha Venturini thought it was pretty funny. Tisha, a world-class header in her own right, started the game going after every airball, just as she always did. Soon, she learned it was useless. "It was hilarious," Tisha says. "We'd both go after all the airballs. Then I finally said, 'I'll just let you take them. You're gonna get them all anyway.'" Michelle's dominance in the air took away Norway's main offensive weapon — long accurate passes from the backs to the front-runners. The first three passes Norway flew in Michelle's direction went off her head and back toward the Norwegian goal.

"Against Norway, she was winning every single head ball," says Carla Overbeck. "I love to have her in the midfield because she is so dominant in the air. Norway plays such a direct style, but Michelle put our defense at ease. We didn't have to worry about winning those balls in the air."

Six minutes and twenty-three seconds into the game, Brandi Chastain went down after a collision, banging her tender left knee. If Chastain was substituted for, she would be lost for the rest of the game. The U.S. coaches and medical staff wanted to see if she could make it back, so they played with ten players until Brandi was able to re-enter the game from the sideline. Eleven minutes later, with Chastain still on the sideline, Norway's Agnete Carlsen intercepted a clearance pass thirty yards out from the U.S. goal. With Carla Overbeck and Tisha Venturini closing fast, Carlsen deftly chipped the ball over the two Americans to Linda Medalen. Medalen, Norway's top striker and one of the best in the world, took the ball off the outside of her right foot, and in stride, placed it under the right hand of the charging Briana Scurry and into the lower left corner of the net. The USA went into the locker room trailing 1-0.

AT HALFTIME, MICHELLE STUMBLED INTO THE LOCKER room and sank to the floor. "I was working on her, and her eyes were rolling in the back of her head," says Steve Slain. "And she was saying 'I can't do it.' I kept saying, 'You will finish! You've got to finish! They need you!'" Tiffeny Milbrett noticed the severity of Michelle's state. "She came off the field into the locker room, ripped her shirt off, grabbed some water, and collapsed in the corner," says Tiffeny. "She didn't move too much. Just laid there. She was probably not sure exactly where she was. She was just trying to recover as fast as she could so she could go out there for another forty-five minutes and push through the pain, letting her mind and body be guided by autopilot. I think she did better when people didn't recognize her zombie-like demeanor. So no one really ever did ... out loud. But everyone was worried for her."

"At the half, I found myself out of energy," Michelle explains. "I laid down on the locker room floor and started praying for the energy and strength to endure. I always try to hide it from the other players. But Steve knew I was struggling, and as usual, he shoved a PowerBar and a Gatorade/water mixture down my throat to fuel the tank. I was miserable and afraid I'd never make it through the game. I knew the second half would be a pure struggle. I was so beat, so absolutely exhausted. But I had done it before so I just concentrated on doing what I could do — win air balls, distribute, get in the box on free kicks. That was my way to contribute to the game."

Michelle pushed on, not only playing but playing well. Kristine Lilly continued her dynamic and crowd-pleasing ventures into the Norwegian end, and with twenty-five minutes gone in the second half, Norway coach Even Pellerud replaced the defender Lilly was abusing with Trine Tangeraas. Ten minutes later, Tangeraas was whistled for a handball in Norway's penalty area — penalty kick USA. Part of Michelle's everyday training program for years included blasting literally hundreds of soccer balls at the goal. Years of hard work and repetition made her shot deadly accurate and perhaps the hardest in the world. But with her energy level low, would she be able to convert the single most important shot of her life? At first, she did not immediately know what was going on. At the time of the call, Michelle was concentrating on making a run to the corner flag, from where the play initiated. On her mind, as it was throughout the Olympics, was the concern about how much energy she was expending on that one particular run. Would it sap her strength? Would she have enough left to finish the game? When the whistle blew for the hand ball, she was wiped out, desperately in need of a rest. She could barely stand anymore, but she wanted that kick. She knew she could tie the game if she got the chance. Sixty-five thousand people waited to see who would take it.

"I looked around to see who else wanted it," Michelle remembers. "Carla Overbeck was off getting water, so she was out. I looked at Brandi Chastain, and she was standing in the back — she was out. I looked to Tony and he pointed at me. So I stepped up to the mark and took the ball. I thought, 'This is the moment I have been waiting for.' I was calm. I was confident. And very aware of the moment and the importance of this PK. If I missed, we would probably lose. I chose to go to my left and decided to drive it as hard as I could, so if the keeper got a hand on it, it would take her into the net with it. I looked right, approached the ball, and then focused only on the ball. I had no doubt I would make it. It went left, the goalkeeper went right, and it was 1-1. I was so excited to be faced with that kind of moment. How many times do you get a chance like that in your life? To be faced with that challenge and to make it was an incredible feeling." Michelle leaped into the air, both arms pumping in delight. Foudy was the first American to arrive, and they were soon mobbed by the rest of the team.

The celebration was short-lived, but it served to pump Michelle full of adrenaline. She was re-charged. When the adrenaline wore off, however, she crashed back to reality. "Sometimes,

In the second half of the semifinal match, Michelle blasted a penalty kick past the Norwegian goalkeeper to tie the game, 1-1.

Photo by Allsport

you would look at her, and she just didn't look right," says Carla Overbeck. "You knew you had to keep telling her, 'Come on, you can do it. We need you!' I knew she was going to make it, though. She's a fighter. Soccer's her life, and this was her dream. Whatever it took, she would get it done." Seriously in need of energy, Michelle went to the sideline. "She came running over to the bench with this desperate look on her face," says Steve Slain. "All she could muster was 'PowerBar. Now!' I always carried three or four PowerBars for her in my pack, and of course my hands were all sweaty and I couldn't rip open the wrapper. The whole bench was laughing as I fumbled with the wrapper and Michelle standing there screaming, 'PowerBar … NOW!' I finally got it to her, and she took off running down the field eating a PowerBar as she goes."

Mia Hamm had been causing the Norwegian defenders problems all day. Her speed and dribbling skills left Norway with little else to do but chop her legs out from under her or wrap their arms around her and pull. She was fouled seven times that day. Mia weaved and sliced through the defense, often ending up face down in the grass for her troubles. Her semi-breakaway with less than four minutes remaining in regulation resulted in the ejection of the Norwegian culprit for dragging her down from behind. The ensuing direct kick and two more chances — one by Lilly and one by Foudy — failed to end the game in regulation.

The game would have to be settled in overtime — sudden-death overtime, or as DiCicco chose to call it, Sudden Victory! The first team to score would advance to the gold medal match. During the break before the first overtime period, the Americans huddled around DiCicco, and laying flat on her back, exhausted in the middle of the huddle was Michelle. "At the end of regulation, I came off and told Steve, 'That's it. There's nothing left,'" Michelle says. "No one else heard me because I didn't want anyone else to know how bad I was. But I thought there was no way I could make it another minute. Steve threw me on the ground and started working on me — shaking my legs, shoving another PowerBar down my throat and pouring more Gatorade in me. He kept telling me, 'Yes, you will do this! You can do this!' The team held the meeting right above my head. I laid on the ground with Steve working on me while I gathered the strength for OT. As the team stacked their hands above me, I prayed for the strength to make it another few minutes, to hold on. Steve pulled me up, hit me on the butt, and told me to go out there and do it. He told me later there was no way he would let me come off the field at that point. I needed to be out there, he said, and my team needed me to be out there."

THE TEAM MARCHED OUT FOR OVERTIME. SOME PLAYERS waved their arms to the crowd, urging them on, asking for noise.

Others got together for last minute words of advice. Michelle just walked to her position, telling herself the familiar words "Just a little longer. Hang in there." With five minutes and twenty-three seconds gone in the first overtime period, Tony DiCicco replaced Tiffeny Milbrett with Shannon MacMillan. MacMillan, a highly successful college striker, had been shifted to midfield for the Olympics. When she entered the game this time, however, it was as a forward. Four minutes and nine seconds after Shannon entered the game, she ended it. On her second touch of the game, MacMillan took a nifty pass from Foudy and slotted it past Nordby.

"Mac scored the goal, and all I could think was, we did it — I did it!" Michelle says. "I had lasted. I believe it was a miracle. It was God's strength that carried me through that match. Doc Adams told me he didn't know how I did it. He said it had to be a miracle. There was no other explanation."

Shannon MacMillan celebrates her goal in sudden-death overtime
Photo by Mike Stahlschmidt

Chapter Twenty-Four

AFTER THE GAME, MICHELLE WAS A COMPLETE MESS. In the first three games, she stayed to enjoy the on-field celebration with her teammates as they hugged, high-fived each other and soaked up the adulation from the crowd. This game, however, it was all she could do to get to the locker room. Looking pale and vacant, Michelle was whisked off the field by Steve Slain. She didn't wave to the fans calling her name. She didn't stop at the throng of reporters near the tunnel. She was then informed that her presence was required at the post-game press conference. Ever aware of the importance of the media to the growth of women's soccer, Michelle, through tears of exhaustion and pain, reluctantly agreed. To get to the media room for the press conference, Michelle had to climb four flights of stairs. Steve Slain, afraid she would collapse, grabbed her by her collar and the waistband of her pants and pushed her up the stairs.

"I could barely manage to change my clothes," Michelle says. "Steve stripped off my shoes, socks, shinguards, and tape while I laid on the floor in the locker room crying. I managed to change while everyone packed my bag for me, and then he carried me to the interviews. I had stopped crying by then and did the interviews. I wonder if they knew how awful I felt." In the interview room, Michelle seemed okay. She was pale and her eyes were glassy, but she produced a smile and gave thoughtful responses to questions she cannot remember to this day. She has no idea what she said.

"I held it together until the locker room, where I collapsed beside my locker and cried. I was just spent, so very tired. I just laid there trying to gather enough of something to just change and get to the bus. I was so happy we had won, so thrilled that I had made it through the game, and so grateful for the gift of those minutes and the strength to endure and play well. But I felt so miserably sick and exhausted I couldn't even walk. The rest of the team headed off to a celebration with friends and family. Me, Steve and the Doc hung out in the training room at the dorm stuffing IVs in my arm. It became a ritual — carry me to the training room, get comfortable on the table, and wait for the IV to take effect. Once I got one in, I stopped crying. The second IV enabled me to meet my family for a few minutes."

BACK AT THE OLYMPIC VILLAGE, MICHELLE WAS TREATED like a queen. At every stop during the Olympics, Steve Slain would meet with the venue chefs and explain Michelle's sensitive diet. All the Olympic chefs took personal pride in preparing food specially for Michelle. In Athens, the head chef of the venue would personally prepare and serve Michelle her meals.

"The chefs were awesome," Michelle says. "Steve helped me arrange things the moment we walked into a new venue. They cooked me gluten-free pancakes with the mix I brought. They made sure there were baked potatoes and plain rice available along with plain steamed veggies, chicken, and hot water for my soups. Anything I needed, they got for me or made for me. It had to be prepared a certain way also — low fat and plain except for spices. No oils, sauces, etc. It had to be broiled, steamed, baked, or barbecued. I noticed how the other girls could just walk in and eat. I had to arrange everything the day or meal before. I often longed to be able to just eat, not have to plan!

"I also packed food for every day trip we went on," she adds. "Anytime we left the compound for practice or whatever, I made sure I had some food and water with me. Just in case. If for some reason Tony changed plans and we were going to be away for a longer period of time, I had to be prepared. So my basic C-rations were PowerBars, water, rice cakes, carrots, and an apple or two. I always had these in my bag and shoe bag, or Steve had them with him if I didn't have room, forgot to pack them or needed more than I anticipated."

The IVs, the food, and the rest all gave Michelle as much strength as she could possibly have. Would it be enough? There was one game left, and then it would be over. Would it end with her on the gold medal platform, or would it be silver? She knew the answer. She was absolutely sure she would stand on the gold medal platform and wave to her dad. So she ate, she drank, and she rested, thought and prayed. "The picture in my head was of me standing on the field after the Norway loss in 1995, realizing my efforts weren't good enough," Michelle says. "That loss was a visible and tangible sum total of my physical battles with CFIDS and injuries, and it was a reminder that I was not strong enough to overcome. I had failed. My will was not enough to conquer the obstacles laid in front of me. I had believed I would be able to do something extraordinary despite my circumstances if I just tried hard enough to pull my team through. But I couldn't. I didn't. Looking back now, the extraordinary part was just being there. But I didn't know that then. The sadness and disappointment of the 1995 World Cup came from knowing that no matter how hard I fought, no one would see that fight or the incredibly huge effort I made just to be there, or the sacrifice my team and I made to play soccer. I did not want that feeling again."

At the workouts on the two off days, Michelle stretched and got her blood flowing a little, but not much else. She got her massages, iced down her injuries and rested some more. She would think about the next game with an odd mixture of excitement and dread. "It's a weird feeling to go into a game knowing full well the condition you'll be in afterward," she says. "You have to want it very bad to play despite the post-game trauma." And she wanted it very badly. She thought about 1991, the feeling she had as a world champion. She re-read old articles and journal entries. She thought about Tony DiCicco's words to the team after they watched the Norwegians accept their '95 awards — "Never forget the feeling we have this night. The margin of victory on the field is so small, but the margin off the field is huge." In 1995, the Norwegians were in the limelight, receiving awards, holding the trophy that belonged to the Americans; the U.S. was in the back of the room, unnoticed, and forgotten. In the gold medal match, Michelle so badly wanted to be the difference. She wanted to perform like the Michelle Akers of old. But she knew that was out of the question. Just stick to the plan, she told herself.

TONY DICICCO REMEMBERED THE LACK OF PRESSURING speed the Americans had against the Chinese in the third game of the tournament, and he took care of it. "I wanted to play with three forwards against the Chinese because they rarely see it," says Tony. "I wanted to play three speed demons up front." So the U.S. coach started MacMillan, Milbrett and Hamm at forward. The midfield consisted of Michelle and Venturini in the middle, Foudy on the right side and, of course, Lilly on the left. Overbeck, Fawcett and Chastain held down the back again. Scurry was in goal ... fully clothed. The crowd — 76,481 — was the largest ever to watch a women's sporting event of any kind anywhere in the world. And it was loud. "The crowds at the first three games were awesome," says Tisha Venturini. "But nothing could compare to the crowd at the final. The whole time we were warming up, I was in awe. I just couldn't believe it. I was so into checking out the crowd, I had to remind myself to concentrate on the game."

The crowd-induced adrenaline nearly paid off early when Milbrett stole the ball and crossed it to Hamm, who shot from thirty yards out. The keeper saved it at the left post. One minute, fifteen seconds had elapsed. The Chinese had some pressure of their own, though. Twice in a two-minute span, Fawcett had to come up big in the box to clear a Chinese chance. Fifteen minutes into the game, Michelle was dead tired. She felt she couldn't continue, but somewhere she found the energy. "I had no business being out there," Michelle says now. "I knew I had nothing left yet managed to remain on the field. I guess I was doing okay because Tony didn't yank me. I know Foudy was yelling at me to hang on, telling me the team needed me. But I was so gone at that point, I could barely register any of it. I was just trying to hang on, which was quite a feat playing the Chinese. They run all day long, and if we didn't have the ball, we were the ones running all day long. It was a miserable game for someone with CFIDS."

Michelle's job against Norway and China was to win balls in the midfield and distribute them quickly and accurately. In the eighteenth minute of the gold-medal game, that's exactly what she did. Tiffeny Milbrett came up with a ball in a crowd and slipped it back to Michelle ten yards behind her. Michelle did what her instincts told her, quickly smacking a brilliantly placed ball with the outside of her right foot. It fell right into the path of Lilly on the left flank. Lilly raced to the penalty area and crossed it into the box. Hamm, sprinting to the penalty kick spot, hit a first-time volley with her right foot that screamed off the keeper's hand and bounced off the left post. And there was Shannon Mac to finish off the rebound.

The U.S. lead was short-lived, however. The Chinese caught the Americans in a defensive breakdown, and Wen Shui chipped a floater over Scurry for the tie with thirteen minutes left in the first half. In the locker room at halftime, Michelle was a mess, a heap of exhaustion, confusion and determination. Steve pumped PowerBars and diluted Gatorade into her and massaged her legs. Michelle would later say that she felt twenty-five times worse than she did after the Norway game. And it was just halftime — a minimum of forty-five minutes still to play. Steve Slain kept telling her that the team needed her, and that she could and would continue. Michelle knew it was true, but she didn't know where she would find the strength. When it was time to go out for the second half, Steve helped her to her feet, and off she went. "I sat next to Tony on the bench," says Steve. "And he kept saying over and over, 'Whatever you do, you'd better tell me when she has to come out. You'd better tell me!' And I was thinking, 'There's no way I'm going to tell him to take her out of this game. There's no way.'"

In the second half, very little registered with Michelle's brain. She could hear Foudy, and she could hear a dull roar from the crowd, but that was it. Another trip to the bench area produced another PowerBar from Steve. Michelle grabbed it, bit off a hunk and returned to the action. Moments later, Michelle stripped a

*Against China
in the Gold Medal game,
the victory for Michelle
was finishing the match.*

Photo by Mike Stahlschmidt

Chinese player of the ball with a half-eaten PowerBar in her hand. "Yes, Mich!," Sue Akers screamed into the viewfinder of her video camera. "Just like Popeye and his spinach." Michelle's feet were working on their own. She would receive passes and quickly send them off to where they needed to go, but she never thought about any of it. It just happened. In the stands, the Akers family contingent screamed for her, prayed for her and silently urged her on. "I watched the video my stepmom put together, and as she watched me in the viewfinder, you could hear her saying, 'C'mon Mee-Mee, hang in there. You can do it,'" Michelle says. "Sad, but so true. It wasn't 'C'mon Mich score another goal' like the tape from '91. It was 'C'mon, hang in there.' For them — and for me — the victory was to make it through the match without killing myself, without having to pay so very dearly for the effort, without having to pay for the desire to win. The victory was being on the field."

With just over nineteen minutes left before overtime, Mia Hamm got the ball on the Chinese half of midfield near the right sideline.

Standing Fast

On Mia's left, Joy Fawcett started a sprint toward the goal. On the far side of the field, Tiffeny Milbrett took off unnoticed into Chinese territory. Mia patiently waited for just the right moment, then threaded a pass between two Chinese players. As she passed the ball, Mia stepped back and watched, providing as much body English as she could muster. On the left flank, Milbrett hit full stride. Joy, the twenty-eight-year-old mother of three-year-old Katelyn Rose Fawcett, out-raced two Chinese defenders and carried the ball into the penalty area. The goalkeeper charged. And at precisely the right moment, Fawcett slipped the ball to Milbrett, who poked it in for the 2-1 lead. Seventy-six thousand, four-hundred and eighty-one fans went berserk. The U.S. players raced around the field in a frenzied celebration; the Chinese sank to their knees. Michelle was just trying to hold on. Now, however, she could see the end. It was eighteen minutes and fifty seconds away. "Everyone has a breaking point, but she never seemed to reach hers," says Foudy. "It's really amazing when you think of it.

Those eighteen minutes were perhaps some of the best soccer the USA played in the entire tournament. China desperately tried to mount an attack. But each time, the Americans turned them back before the threats became dangerous. Instead of just booting the ball aimlessly down field and out of danger, the U.S. maintained possession and patiently ran out the clock. With seventy-six thousand anxiously awaiting the referee to blow the whistle three times to signal the end of the match, Carin Gabarra chased a loose ball toward the Chinese goal. The ref blew the whistle ... then blew it again. The third whistle was drowned out by the huge roar from the crowd. It was over. Gold Medal, USA. "The last minutes were agonizing," says Michelle. "I watched the clock tick down and waited and waited for the whistle. It seemed to take forever. But finally, the game was over, and God had given me a truly miraculous experience and a very special gift. It was more relief and gratefulness than anything else. It was over! We had done it. I had done it. Now I could rest."

The players soaked in the adulation and thanked every corner of Sanford Stadium for the support. Kristine Lilly raced to the bench to get her camera. Carla Overbeck grabbed her camcorder.

The FBI formed a ring around the field. Steve Sampson, the men's national team coach, was at the fence with his camera. The DiCicco family came down out of the crowd to wait for their dad. Michelle hugged everyone she could find. She carried a flag and blew kisses to the crowd. For the moment, she was not someone suffering from CFIDS, or a complete physical and emotional mess. She was a world champion. And she felt great. During the on-field celebration, every time Michelle turned around there was another world champion smiling ear-to-ear, ready to be hugged. There was Julie and Kristine and Mia, players that Michelle watched get their driver licenses at age sixteen. There was Carla and Carin and Joy and Brandi and Mary Harvey, with whom Michelle celebrated five years earlier in China. There was Tisha and Tiffeny and Mac and Bri, relative newcomers to the team but so important to Michelle. There were Tiffany Roberts, Cindy Parlow and Staci Wilson, the youngsters and future of a team Michelle helped build. Racing in from the sidelines, were the four alternates — Jen Streiffer, Thori Staples, Saskia Webber and Amanda Cromwell.

There is a photo taken during the gold medal ceremony that describes the relationship shared by the players. The sixteen players are on the medal platform wearing their medals and holding their flowers. The camera is nearly in front of them, but all sixteen heads are turned to the left. They are looking left because that's where the alternates, coaches and staff are snapping their personal photos. "The memories and experiences from the Olympics are less about winning and more about people," says Michelle. "I learned that all of us — fans, family, friends, chefs, volunteers, police, politicians, officials, sponsors — are part of the team. It took all of us to prepare and to win. The Olympic Games are about conquering obstacles. It's about incredible passion, fire and desire. It is about unity and love and achieving a dream. It is about becoming more than you are. And by reaching for our dreams, we inspired others to reach for theirs."

THE PLAYERS FINALLY CLEARED THE FIELD, RETURNING TO the locker room to change and await the medal ceremony. "I was one of the first ones back into the locker room," says Tisha Venturini. "I got to see everyone come in, and those were the happiest faces I've ever seen. But Michelle was just laid out on the floor."

The team changed and then went back into the tunnel to wait for the ceremonies to begin, lining up numerically. "When we were waiting to come out of the tunnel, Michelle was dazed and she could hardly stand," remembers Julie Foudy. "I was lined up next to her, because she's number ten and I'm number eleven, and she finally had to sit down. She was a mess." Mia Hamm, number nine, leaned down and told Michelle the familiar words, "Just a little longer. You can do it." The players entered the field to roars from the crowd, and as they made the long walk to the medal platform, Michelle, with a blank look on her face, searched the stands. Suddenly, she found her family and raised both arms in an excited wave. The blank look turned to an immense smile. After the bronze was awarded to Norway and the Silver to China, the USA took their places on the medal platform. First, captain Carla Overbeck received her medal from International Olympic Committee President Juan-Antonio Samarach and flowers from United States Soccer Federation President Alan Rothenberg. Next Scurry, Harvey, Parlow, Roberts, Chastain, Wilson, MacMillan, Hamm and then Michelle. "This is a moment many dream about ... and it's exactly as you imagine it," says Michelle. "Almost sur-real. Extremely emotional. Tears, laughter, disbelief, joy — all at once, and all very overwhelming." As each player received their medal, they immediately checked it out, reading the inscription, showing it off to the crowd, giving it a kiss. The first thing Michelle noticed about her medal was it seemed very heavy. She just took a deep breath and let out a sigh of relief.

When the team finally left the field, they headed back through the tunnel, and Michelle realized it was over. When they got back into the locker room, the team was whipped up into a frenzy, cel-ebrating their triumph. "Michelle certainly wasn't going crazy like the rest of us," says Mary Harvey. "She was sitting there, just exhausted, but she had this satisfied look on her face. It's hard to explain. She was subdued, but she looked completely satisfied."

Colleen Hacker asked twice if she could take Michelle's picture. It seemed to be such a poignant moment, a complete contrast to what the public saw and a total departure from the bedlam of the locker room. "She was just lying there on the floor, completely spent," says Colleen. "I mean there was nothing left. Absolutely nothing. She was just lying there, dazed and totally content, a mixture of peace and accomplishment. And then she held up her gold medal."

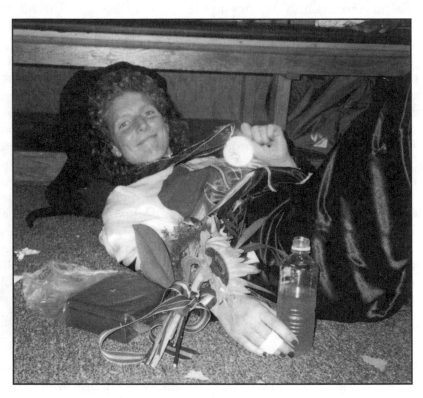

Photo by Colleen Hacker

Chapter Twenty-Five

NIKE HAD RENTED A SORORITY HOUSE IN ATHENS FOR post-game receptions. Lisa Gozley and Laurie (Hayden) Trevers waited there for an hour and a half to see Michelle after the gold medal game. When she finally arrived, whispers of "Michelle's here!" circulated the house. "Michelle walked in, looking like a zombie," Lisa says. They chatted briefly before Michelle had to leave, but Michelle never mentioned just how sick she was to her two college friends. She had never told them the extent of her illness and the details of her struggle. It wasn't until the next day that Gozley finally became aware of the severity of Michelle's illness.

"We were at a post-game party, and her stepmom was passing out little cards with Michelle's CFIDS testimony on it," remembers Lisa. "It had her picture on it, so I thought it was a soccer card or something. I threw it in my pocket. The next day on the plane, I got it out and read it. I started crying. It was describing her day and what she had gone through. It upset me for a couple days. I called her, and we had a long conversation. I was part angry that she didn't tell me and part hurt because I felt I had been a bad friend. She tried to explain to me that for a long time, she really didn't understand it either, and that she didn't want to bother us because there was really nothing we could do. I told her she was wrong, and that we could have helped her if she'd told us. I didn't understand it at all. I worried about her a lot. She kept everything inside her because she never wanted anyone to worry about her. She never wanted to burden anyone. I would ask her if she was all right, and she'd just say, 'I'm fine.'"

Kristine Lilly was a quiet teenager when she first joined the national team as an immensely talented sixteen-year-old. It was hard for her to get to know the veterans. The first thing she noticed, though, was how Michelle punished her body for the team. Nine years later, it was no surprise to Kristine and the other veterans that Michelle did it again. Mia Hamm explained to reporters at the Olympics that punishing her body is how Michelle shows the team that she loves them. Mia and Kristine were among those who marveled at the dedication and focus Michelle displayed throughout. At times, they worried about her, and at times they wondered why Michelle would put herself through all the pain and sacrifice. "I think whenever people get an illness, it's because they have the strength to deal with it," says Kristine. "It's almost like a test to see if you still have it in you. And Michelle's illness affected her — and many others — in such a positive way. It showed people that she was not this Superwoman. It showed that she was human. People could talk to her about something other than soccer, talk to her on a more personal level."

Michelle's emotional struggle was perhaps more difficult than the physical battle she waged. Sometimes it took everything she had just to appear normal, when in truth she wanted to crawl under a rock and die. And yet, she got dressed, went to practice, joked with her buddies, took free kicks, ran sprints, and no one knew the difference ... until she had to sit out. "Mentally, it was absolutely exhausting to fight my body to appear normal and then have to play soccer at the highest level," she says. "It tires me out just thinking about it. The more I think back, the more I come to realize how incredibly hard each day was for me. But you see, I was willing to go through all that to play soccer with those people and to be a part of the best team in the world."

In the end, Michelle discovered it was those personal aspects of her journey that mattered most. It was her relationships with friends, family and teammates that were most important. All the struggles were very much worthwhile, not for the shiny medal around her neck, but the manner in which it was achieved. She competed against herself and her illness for perfection, for excellence and for the sheer challenge of testing herself. With the help of God, she was able to face the challenges and push herself to the edge. She didn't back down, and of that she was very proud.

The thrill she enjoyed came from finding she had enough inside her, discovering she had the guts to keep going when she wanted to quit. But the real satisfaction was the feeling she shared with her teammates, family and friends. It was an emotion so few knew, the feeling of utter satisfaction and accomplishment, the feeling of a world champion. And she felt the immense power of God in her and the peace and serenity that accompanied it. "I truly don't know how I did it," she says. "Of course, God is the only explanation."

Chapter Twenty-Six

August 2, 1996.

I T'S THE DAY AFTER THE GOLD MEDAL GAME. MY *thoughts are scattered and disjointed, but the sentiment and unforgettable memories will forev-er be embedded in my heart. My mind keeps returning to the past few years where I thought I was so alone, so isolated in my struggles and pain. God is so good. Through it all, He was preparing me for this moment, this experience. So very faithful. He took it all away, but He gave me back so much more. (Eph 3:19-20).*

Tonight, I go to bed an Olympic Champion.

Epilogue

ON AUGUST 23, 1996, 22 DAYS AFTER WE WON THE GOLD, Medal I visited a woman named Cheryl who is sick with cancer. She's dying. She is close to the end. What a humbling experience for me. I showed her the Gold Medal and she just lit up. I will never forget her face or the way she struggled to hold it herself ... but could not because she was too weak. So sad, but so inspiring.

Again, the Gold Medal teaches me something. It has become a story, a part of me to share. The commitment, the desire, the guts and the blood molded into the shape of a medal that allows people to touch and feel hope, achievement and an overcoming spirit. The medal allows people to look at the idea of the summit and the possibility of reaching a dream. They can touch and hold the reality of it.

If I can do it   so can you.

It is the reality of a dream that was formed long ago. The reality of many intangibles — pain, effort, sacrifice, choices, priorities, and prayer. All those quiet things done over the course of years, many times a day, built to an achievement that people can start to understand. I say "start" because only I can ever know what it took for me to be an Olympian. To be a Gold Medalist. To be Michelle Akers.

CFIDS took away who I was for a time. It took away what I did. And it almost took away my hope and belief that I could change the world, that I could make a difference. After five years of battling the illness and trying to maintain my status on the U.S. National Team, I finally gave up. I fell on my knees and cried to God — I can't do this anymore. I give up. I have no more strength. And God took me (with CFIDS) and did something amazing. He turned my suffering, my illness into a blessing and a miracle. Yes, you heard me right — CFIDS has been my blessing. It has enabled me to find out who I am. It has made me more than I was before I got sick. It has made me powerful and strong.

I have learned, and I absolutely believe, God put me — and you — here to allow others to share in our struggle and our wisdom. I sat in the hospice room with Cheryl and her grieving family and was changed. Yes, I have a Gold Medal, but she was more powerful, more moving than any trophy or title I could ever achieve. She was powerless, and yet she touched me in an extremely powerful way. She was weak — too weak to even lift the Gold Medal. And yet, her strength was, and still is, evident in her life, her death, her family, and now, me.

Cancer is a terrible disease. CFIDS is a devastating illness. But, I thank and praise God for the circumstances and the struggle I went through for the opportunity to meet Cheryl. If neither one of us had been sick, our paths would never have crossed. I would never have known the meaning of real suffering and the impact of reaching out because of loss and pain. I have a Gold Medal to help tell my story. I challenge you to find your Gold Medal. Over time and fruitless searching, this challenge will become a journey, and this journey will eventually lead you to the truth — that a Gold Medal may open the door, but all you really have to show or to give is you.

In reality, that is all I bring to you — myself. And you know what? That is all that is needed. That's enough. It is all God requires of us to give to Him, and it is all we can ultimately give to each other. We all share in the ability to transcend illness, struggle, and even death by making it something worthwhile. Something life-changing. Something powerful. I did it. Cheryl did it. And so can you.

God bless and good health.

Michelle

Appendix A

Cast of Characters

Mark Adams: Doc Adams. He came on board and made a huge impact on me. So very nice, and yet so established and respected. On his first road trip with the team, he pulled me aside and expressed his concern and desire that he contribute to the team in the best possible way. He asked if I had any suggestions, and I was knocked back. My first thought was, 'Wow, he'll fit right in!' And he did. When he wasn't fixing someone up, he was chasing balls, carrying gear, or helping out with laundry.

Doc. Adams (left) and Steve Slain

Doc Adams and I spent a lot of time together. Before and during the Olympics, I was a high-maintenance player, always hurt or sick. I needed lots of work. And you know what? He never balked or blew me off. He was always there when I needed him, and even more than that, he believed in me. I could trust him. He researched ways to help fend off CFIDS and NMH, called my docs, read up on the latest available treatments. He worked his butt off for me. He's another one who walked in and made an immediate impact on the strength and power of the team. He not only did his job exceedingly well, but contributed as a person to the team. He gave himself, and in turn, was an integral part of the team winning the Gold.

Dr. James Barnett: Doc B. Doctor Barnett and I have known each other for quite some time now. In fact, he has done the majority of my knee surgeries and is always the first one I call (along with Rodney Negrete, my PT) when I return to Orlando from the National Team in need of repair. He is one of the country's best orthopedic docs, and I have the luxury of also knowing he is one of the nicest and most generous people you will ever come across. He is the greatest and deserves as much of the Gold Medal as anyone in this section. He earned it.

159

Doc Brown

Dr. Doug Brown: DB. Another Doc B is another great Doc. He wasn't allowed to come to the Olympics with us because of some USOC rule, but he has been our Doc for at least two years now. He was with us in Sweden and even before on many, many road trips. Before that, he traveled with the men's national team so he was pretty experienced in patching up soccer players. He is the greatest, and his wife, Margs is awesome too.

Doc B, like Doc Adams, adds to the team more than just being our doctor. He adds to us as a *person*. He is another one who does it all — laundry, food runs, ball-chasing, up in the middle of the night for a diarrhea emergency, stitches in the locker room, singing. You name it he does it well ... singing, maybe not so good.

Anyway, although DB couldn't be with us on the field at the Olympics, he was in our hearts and had already made his indelible mark on us in our preparation to win the Gold. His influence and friendship have been tremendous.

Brandi Chastain: Brandi. She's been around for a while, too. Some think she has just recently burst onto the scene, but she played in the '91 World Cup and has played in Japan for a couple years as well. Brandi is an exceptional player and a true soccer junky. She plays soccer, watches soccer, coaches soccer, reads about soccer, sleeps soccer. She loves soccer. We can be in the midst of a hellish camp, training two times a day, totally immersed in soccer, exhausted and burnt, and she will want to go watch a game. Nuts.

Brandi is a good friend. We have a lot in common. We have had a long run of knee surgeries. Between us, we have probably rebuilt six-to-ten totally brand new knees. She is also one of the early risers on the team. I wake up around 6:00 a.m. (sometimes earlier) and usually go the lobby of the hotel or cafeteria and drink coffee and read until it's breakfast time. Then I join the rest of the team who have literally just dragged themselves out of bed. By that time, I am totally wired with four-fifty cups of coffee in me. Well, Brandi is an early riser

*Brandi Chastain
and her buddies from the Olympics.*

too. So, we began the routine of hanging out before breakfast, chatting about the news, and deep philosophical life questions. I really enjoy our little morning time together.

Lastly, it's a little known fact that Brandi is a great cook. She can definitely whip up some tasty meals. Sometime last year, we began the tradition of having a lobster feast at my place. We chose lobster because it wasn't an every day kind of food, and it was on my gluten-free, dairy-free, everything-tasty-except-lobster-free diet. Regular attendees were Brandi, as master chef and overall coordinator, Mac, Millie, myself as host, Sal, and CP (you'll figure out the nicknames as you read along). We fixed lobster (prepared at Goodings grocery store), butter with garlic and lemon, a big salad, and mashed potatoes. We chowed! Those were the days. I can't wait for our next residency period.

Amanda Cromwell: Sal. Sally Mally Wally Jally. As you can see we go off on our nicknames for each other. Sal is just another National Team nickname victim. And there

Michelle and Amanda Cromwell.

are many of us! Sal was one of those friends that kind of sneaks up on you. One minute, I barely knew her. The extent of our relationship was kicking the hejeebers out of each other on the field. And the next thing you know, I am cooking her dinner and hanging out.

The basis of our friendship is soccer, yes, but we have a real family-type of love for each other. I even hang out with her Granny Fay and Grandpa Bill, and I'm known as the "new granddaughter." Sal and I have a great affinity for arguing with each other. It's her gift. She can pick any subject and get me all riled up to the point where I have to say "I'm not talking to you anymore." It's that sisterly love kind of thing, I guess.

Anyway, I was happy to have Sal as my roommate in Sweden, because I had some tough stuff hit me. She really rallied for me when I was out of it with the concussion and the knee, and she became a real friend in a time of need. God answered one of my prayers when He placed Sal in my close circle of friends.

Tony DiCicco: Tony. I can tell you his nickname after one of us retires. So for now anyway, it will have to remain in the family. Tony came to us as a goalkeeper coach. When Anson retired, he took over. I like training with Tony because he gets down and dirty with the players ... especially at keeper practice. He jumps in goal and dives all over the place in whatever kind of weather and field conditions. I love that. I mean,

Tony and Diane DiCicco

how many times do you get to whack shots at your coach or send him sprawling in the mud?

One story comes to mind that I'm sure Tony will recall with some ... shall we say trepidation. It was just before the Olympics, and we were practicing free kicks during a scrimmage. The ball was stopped dead inside the box and we had an indirect kick. Well, the team lines up the wall and Tony jumps in goal (to save Bri from the chance of injury) and warns me to aim close to him so no one else gets hurt. So I line up to take the shot, and I nail him. Not once, but twice. And not kind of hard, but hard. I hit him once in the arm and once, well, you know, in the uh ... midsection. After that last one, well, that was the end of that. I don't think he'll be doing that again soon. So you see, Tony is willing to go the extra mile, and of course, we are all appreciative.

Anson Dorrance: Anson. The name evokes so many feelings amidst the soccer community. How so many people see and feel about Anson really cracks me up. It seems either you love him or you hate him. Anson recruited me as a skinny little girl out of Seattle. I was not impressed. In fact, I did not like Anson. I said that in an interview a couple years back and Anson's Mom got all mad at me. Yes, I hated Anson at first, but as the years passed and his Tar Heels continually pounded UCF and me, I grew to respect him. And then, to my surprise, we struck up a great friendship.

I learned a lot from him over the years about a great many things. I learned what it means to train for the National Team. What it means to be fit. That detail and precision is an important thing in the game of soccer. How to motivate players. And how to play the politics with the mucky mucks. Anson built the basis of how the current National Team operates and wins by, even now. Prepare and train on our own. Be committed to the one thing you can control — your fitness. Be smart and be aware that your decisions and actions on and off the field effect the team. Sell the game. Play for each other. Compete with intensity, respect, and guts. Train and play on the edge. We represent the USA — be proud of that and make the USA proud of us.

Tracy (Noonan) Ducar: Noons is one of our goalkeepers. Poor Noons injured her back pretty severely just prior to the Olympics which forced her out of the running for a spot on the team. I was so sad for her because she (as all of us on the team) worked so hard for so long and then, to have an injury so close to the Games was really tough. She handled it like a pro though, and kept up a good attitude, even though she had to be dying inside.

I have a funny story about Noons and her now husband, Chris Ducar. Tracy proposed to Chris in Orlando in one of my favorite restaurants (Colorado Fondue). She told us her plans and arranged it with Blake, the owner of the restaurant (and friend of mine), so there was a big build up to it. When it was finally over and she reported the details of her big night at practice the next day, we all celebrated with her. Weeks later, I was chatting with some guys from SoccerPlus Goalkeeper School (Tony's camps). As par for the course, I couldn't remember where I knew these guys from. I was sure I knew them from somewhere, but for the life of me, I could not figure out where. So I kept talking, figuring eventually I would dredge up their faces and names from somewhere in that hazy memory of mine. Anyway, like an idiot, I told them about Noonan's surprise proposal, and guess who the guy was ... Chris, her fiancé. Boy, did I feel like a jerk. I know I'll never hear the end of that one.

Joy Fawcett: Beef. We call her Beef because of her maiden name, Biefeld, not because she is fat or beefy or anything like that. We also call her Wonder Woman because she is just plain awesome. Just to show you how modest and unassuming Beef is about her talent, she still fears for her position and place on the team. Honest! She comes off the field and sometimes says she hopes Tony doesn't cut her because she stunk it up out there.

If you think that's incredible, get a load of this. She had Katie (her first child) and was on the field within four weeks of giving birth. Yikes! How's that for a little inspiration? And then, Katie came everywhere with us ... in the U.S., out of the country, in the hotels, wherever we went, Katie went. Beef took care of her and played full time. The

Joy and Katie Fawcett

baby experience has been a good thing for me. Although I wasn't sure about the baby stuff at first, I am now, at least, not afraid of them. It took a few months before I would hold Katie and then, as she got to know the team and me, my fears and uncertainty melted away. Katie is awesome. She calls me Moofasa, and I play house with her sometimes. We are still not best buds, but I know deep down I am probably one of her favorites.

So, back to Mama Beef. Joy is the fittest or one of the fittest on this team. She has asthma too, so that should bring some inspiration to those who think they can't have asthma and play soccer. Joy does it and so can you. I love playing with Beef because she's so steady and so good. She never misses a step. She just kind of slips in, takes the ball from the best player on the opposing team, and then passes it up field, or simply takes it up there herself. Nothing flashy or fancy, just world-class steadiness. Beef is like that in real life too. A world-class person.

Eva Ferara: Eva and I have been working together since 1991. At first, she was my rep within Umbro. After she left them, she became my business manager. Eva was one of the first to push and encourage Umbro to sign a female and pay more attention to women's soccer. They, of course, resisted the idea of a female endorsee for quite a while ... until, at last, Mick Hoban came in and changed everything.

I came into Umbro as a kid. Although I had talent and showed promise, I was very rough around the edges. Over the years, Eva has helped me evolve into an adult who is still rough, but now, at least, I am better equipped to be a spokesperson of sorts. I still get in trouble because I work from my heart more than is politically correct. But Eva provides a nice balance to that stubborn, maverick side of me. She is one of those pioneers you don't get to read about because she is behind the scenes.

Julie Foudy: Fouds and Lil came on the team as these skinny, little girls. I remember looking at them and thinking they can't even drive yet. But, they were good. They were a bit intimidated and easy to throw off the ball, but showed great promise.

Foudy was Miss Personality, even when she was fifteen. And Loud. Loudy Foudy is one of her nicknames. I can remember thinking, "Who is this girl? Does she ever shut up? How

Julie Foudy and Michelle

does so much noise come out of one person's mouth?" You could always tell which floor Foudy was on ... it was always the loudest in the hotel. All kidding aside, Foudy has proved to be a spark, a fire, for the team. When she is not there, the team is definitely not the same. She is full of an exuberance for the game and for life that is unmatched. And when she is on the field, she encourages, challenges, and inspires us all at the same time. And thank God for that because many, many times, Foudy was the one who provided that small push to keep me going when I thought for sure I couldn't take another step.

Carin Gabarra: Gumby and I go way back. But before I go on maybe I should explain why she's called Gumby. She is pigeon-toed. And when she runs or falls, she gets all contorted and Gumby-like. Hence, the name Gumby. Anyway, as I was saying, she is a world-class veteran and a great friend. Here's a story for you: On one tour to China, Gumby and I were roommates, and I suffered a concussion during one of the matches. I was really out of it. After I had kind of recovered, she walked into the room one afternoon and I said to her, "Hey, check out this book. Have you read it? It's really good!" And she just laughed at me. Apparently, in my concussion fog, I had picked up her book and made it my own.

Carin and Jim Gabarra

She let me finish it, although I have never heard the end of it to this day.

In fact, Gumby — the entire team for that matter — are always quick to point out my mistakes and stupidities. And believe me, there are lots of opportunities. I do lots of stuff that continually keeps the team — especially the vets — laughing. None of it on purpose. Just typical Akers stuff. One of Gumby's nicknames for me is "Epstein." Her, Fouds and Carla would always yell at me to get off the field, "Hey Epstein! Go sit down, you've had enough!" Those three plus Sal and Steve (Slain) are my primary watch dogs on the field.

Lisa Gozley: Goz is one of my best friends. She loves to psychoanalyze everything, so I am the perfect friend/subject for her. She spends hours digging into my psyche trying to figure out what makes me tick. And then, we do it to everyone around us. It's

Laurie Trevers, Michelle and Lisa Gozley

pretty funny. On the outside, we look like we're from different worlds, but our hearts are much the same.

Goz is married now. In fact, she is living in the very place she made so much fun of when we were in college together — good ole Washington State. But she's not even living in Seattle, a big city. She lives in Pullman (coaching at Washington State University)

165

which is on the east side of the state and total farm country. Look who's Betty Crocker now! Anyway, her husband Larry (another cocky New Yorker) is always challenging me to a game of 1v1 — him in goal and me shooting from the top of the box. He thinks he can beat me. I have just one thing to say to Larry ... Wake up dude! Did you get run over by a cow or something and lose touch with reality?

Laurie Gregg: Laurie played for Anson in college and is therefore, Anson-educated. For all of you who have played for Anson, you know what I mean. She is a thorough and detailed coach, and I believe her strength to be in scouting, pre-game preparation talks, tactics, video and match analysis. She is the brains behind the team. She takes care of details — an invaluable job.

On a personal side, Laurie has been chronically ill for quite some time and although, she never discusses it and has never gone public with it, I have encouraged her to share her story. She has endured and accomplished so much that if you knew her full story, you would no doubt be inspired. She and I have had the opportunity to talk about the effects of chronic illness and it has allowed me to see just how prevalent the stuff I went through is in chronically sick people. She is now coaching the Under-20 National Team and is on staff as our assistant as well.

Colleen Hacker: Hack. Or more accurately HACKER! I always have to yell it at her when I see her. Hack came to us at a point when we desperately needed it. The team as a whole was in need of an positive outside influence, and I found out she would be a powerful ally to me on a personal level as well.

Because my Dad is a shrink and I am familiar with "shrink tactics," I was wary of her tactics and of her at first. I thought, how could this lady help our team? What does she know? Well, boy was I pleasantly surprised. We loved her, and if she hadn't been so great, we would not have won those Olympics. Yes, she is that great. Not that we are a bunch of

Colleen Hacker

whackos and psychotics, but she added a dimension that was desperately needed prior to the Games. She gave us a safe place and a safe person to vent fears, anxieties and personal stuff to without feeling threatened.

The Olympics is a big thing and the commitment to train for them is a big thing. It's tough at times, and to know you had someone there to listen impartially without threat was invaluable. Many took advantage of her ability to help concentration and focus. Others, to increase confidence, or even ways to deal with stuff amongst the team and coaching staff. I benefited from her because I finally had someone to talk with who was a part of the team and our quest ... and yet, not part of the team. It was important to keep the illness away from my team and staff, and therefore, I got stuck with a lot of "stuff" that was very hard to deal with. I had to keep a lot inside. Hacker helped me vent, offered ways to deal with the uncertainty and difficulty of CFIDS and soccer. She was available in a heartbeat to run errands or do stuff for me that I couldn't burden my team with on the road. She is cool, and I consider her a good friend. She is very loving, giving, and almost childlike in her passion for the team and our quest to be the best.

Mia Hamm: Hammer. It has been fun watching Mia grow up in the game. She has worked so hard to transform herself into one of the best players in the world, and we are glad the world is taking notice. On top of that, it has been truly exciting to see Nike take her and run! Go Hammer!

A lot of people wonder (but, rarely do they ask up front) how I feel when she is called "The best player in the world," like she stole it from me or something. I want everyone to know ... I am so proud of her. It is a great thing. She has worked so hard for it. We have worked as hard for it alongside her. People need to understand that whatever one of us accomplishes, it's reason for all of us to celebrate. Her success is our success. The better each of us does, the better for all and the better for the game. One for all and all for one is truly our team creed.

Mary Harvey: Harv or Harvina. Another nickname victim. Harv is a vet. She has been on the team for a while and has played pro in Germany for many years. The thing I admire about Harv is her heart. She works hard, she busts butt every single day. And she has that same attitude toward everyone off the field as well. She will go the extra mile if you are in need. Harv struggled the past couple years with injuries, and I watched her leave the field many times in tears of frustration. Pain and injury hurts both in body and heart, and when you've had a few injuries on a continual basis it gets a little old. The cool thing about Harv is she never gave up. She kept on going even when she wanted to quit and even when everyone would have understood if she quit.

One of those injuries was to her wrist and it was a really nagging, painful injury. Many times, she would block a hard shot and explode in pain, and then have to leave the field with a huge bag of ice on her wrist. Well, our trainer got her a splint thing that kinda looked like a glove. It held her wrist stiff and added support in order to prevent it from bending backward. Well Millie and I were all over that. We were calling her the Hawk

Woman and asking her when her hawk was gonna come down and land. From then on she'd walk around the field with her arm (and brace) in the air above her head, calling for her trained-killer hawk. We did it almost every practice, and each time Millie and I would laugh harder and harder while the rest of the team looked at us like we were nuts. See. So little entertains us, sometimes it scares even me!

April Heinrichs: Ape is a special person, player and leader. She is unlike anyone I have ever met. In fact, to this day, I am still trying to figure her out. I played with her in the '91 World Cup and then was coached by her in '95 and '96. Because Ape is a leader, it's hard to get to know her. I think I see a little of myself in her in that respect. When we played together, I generally steered clear of her. She was too intimidating and fierce for the likes of me as youngster. I used to marvel at her competitiveness and intensity. And when she got fired up, I was glad I was on her team. I knew I had grown into my own when one practice session the ball went over the line and she kept playing. I began yelling at her that it was out and it was our throw-in. She argued back, and a yelling match ensued. It was fun. Afterward, I kinda laughed about it because here we are getting all riled up over a stupid throw-in on some obscure practice field in France. I knew I was coming into my own when I had the confidence and courage to take on Ape in a yelling match.

When Ape retired, it was hard for us at first. She had always been such a force, and we would miss her enthusiasm and leadership. Her transition from player to coach for the team was smooth and everyone was psyched to have her. I was a little unsure, however. I wasn't sure she was ready, and I didn't know how I would handle her as a coach. I mean, Jeez, I had just gotten used to her as a player. I wasn't disappointed, though. In fact, I wish she had more responsibility, and I often asked her for insight and suggestions as to better ways to do my job up front or in the midfield. Ape has a rare ability to bring the intensity and focus she had as a player onto the field as a coach. It is fun to play for her. She is challenging and tough, but at the same time we have a blast. She is gonna be big time.

Mick Hoban: Mick is a visionary. He is the one who heard me speak to a bunch of soccer investors and business people (at a SICA meeting) after we qualified for the '91 World Cup. He was the one who initially pursued me to sign with Umbro. I'd like to take this opportunity to set the record straight once and for all. Mick Hoban was the first in the corporate world to see the potential of the women's game and then take the risk of doing something that had never been done before. He stepped out in front to lead the soccer world into a new era. He signed and promoted a female player.

Standing Fast

I go to Mick for advice often because I always seem to find myself in situations that are extremely delicate, highly flammable, and involve the integrity and growth of the sport. It is hard not to get fired up when I see something happening that directly affects the team I love and my sport. He (and my dad) are my voices of reason. I trust Mick implicitly. He is full of wisdom, has a genuine passion of the game, and is true of character. So true, in fact, that at one point or another, his stance has cost him jobs, friendships, positions and basically ticked lots of people off because he won't just go with the flow. I like that. I respect that. There aren't too many of those around these days.

I sat with Mick at the 1997 NSCAA Convention in Nashville and watched many people and many companies promote and declare themselves the leaders or innovators of the women's game. I know otherwise. Mick knows otherwise. And yet he sits quietly in the knowledge that he was the force. He was the one who started the whole thing in the first place. You know what? Sadly, not one person or organization has ever stopped to thank him or stopped to recognized the incredible thing he made real for all of us way back in 1991. It's a shame. Why hasn't anyone made note of this man and his place in the game? I don't know. Well, I do know, but it would be politically incorrect to say it. So with all that said, my purpose with these statements is merely to give a public acknowledgment of Mick's courage to go after it. Thank you Mick. I know it isn't on the front page of the paper or headline news for ESPN sports, but I hope in some small way, this, and the state of the game as it is today, is some consolation for all you have done and stood for.

Kristine Lilly: Lilly (nickname pronounced Lee-Lee) came to the team as this quiet, self-composed little girl from Wilton, Conn. She never said much, and I never spent much time with her. The only time I heard anything come out of her mouth was when she hung out with Gumby. And then I thought, "Wow, she's funny. I should hang out with her more often." But I never did. It took me quite a while to know Lil, but she has a special place in my heart. Always so consistent, selfless, and confident. Steady. And she is so dang good. In my opinion, she's one of the best in the world. I love watching her and playing alongside her on the National Team. She is a true stud, and I am full of admiration for her.

Lil always catches me doing something nutty, too. I don't know what it is about her, but I'll

Kristine Lilly

169

find myself doing something stupid and look up, hoping no one saw or heard what I said, and she'll be looking at me. And then she'll start laughing at me. And to shoot down her little "I will never catch her on the speed ladder" comment ... Look out Lil! You'll be lookin' at my backside the next time I race you!

Shannon MacMillan: Mac had a fairy tale Olympics — off the bench and into the pages of history. I was so happy for her (and happy for myself because the sooner she scored, the sooner I could rest). She has agonized and fought hard, especially over the past three years, to be a part of this team. And then, the best possible scenario happened for her.

Tiffeny Milbrett: Millie. What a great story. I saw Millie get on this team when she wasn't so sure about what kind of player she wanted to become. She had to really search for her desire and willingness to do what it takes to be on this National Team. Just prior to the '95 World Cup, she made her choice, and none too soon. She became an integral part of our team in the 95 World Cup and beyond. I have sincerely enjoyed watching her develop into one of our premier goal scorers ... despite her taking my position!

We have a special friendship. I feel like the older sister. We juice veggies together, drink Starbuck Coffee, talk about life, soccer, and laugh a lot. She's a riot. She's the kind of person that is funny without realizing it, which makes her twice as funny, if you know what I mean. She is one of those people who just blurts out the first thing that comes into her head without thinking twice about the consequences or repercussions of the comment. It's great. I like to just sit back, watch, listen, and laugh. The thing I love about Millie is you always know where you stand, and she is who she is. What you see is what you get. I love that.

Tiffeny Milbrett

Rodney Negrete, PT: Rod—neeeeeyyyy. I have lots and lots of nicknames for Rodney. As I come to think of it, it would be great pay back for all the torture he has put me through (and enjoyed entirely too much) over the past couple years. But since I am one of the nicest people I know, I will only give you a couple. Rodney The Great. And Agent Rodney (we are both Mission Impossible movie fans). The others will have to wait. You're welcome, Rodney. You can stop sweating now.

Standing Fast

About Rodney. He is also the greatest. A great physical therapist (PT), a great person, and a great friend. Plus his wife, Deb is cool too. They are the perfect couple. Totally in love and totally falling all over themselves for each other. If I wasn't so jealous and admiring of their relationship, I would probably puke at the amount of love and gooeyness that passes between them.

Rod and I spend many hours a day together trying to strengthen, stretch, and heal my beat-up body. We have a blast together, and even though he is always devising new and ingenious ways to

Rodney and Michelle

torture and break me, I love every minute of it. We laugh at the pain (easy for him to do!) But as I walk out, I'm already looking forward to the next day of work. He has the perfect balance between pushing me and saving me from overdoing it. I can trust him completely. He is a major reason I was able to play in the Olympics. My knee was so thrashed, a doctor (not any in this section) told me I needed reconstruction in order to play. Between Doc Barnett and Rodney, we patched things up enough so I could be on the Gold Medal Team. Oh yeah, the other dudes at Florida Hospital Rehab are pretty cool too. Even you, Eddie.

Carla Overlapper (Overbeck): Carla is a stud. She is a great leader and a great motivator. Carla is someone who makes you want to live up to her expectations and standards — which are exceptional. She came onto the team as a skinny, scrawny girl, but has developed herself into a fitness machine. She is very strong, has incredible endurance both aerobically and anaerobically, and her mental tenacity is extremely intense and focused. She will not accept anything but the best from herself or anyone else around her. And playing alongside her, motivates you to give it all you have. Carla is not only a great leader by example, but by voice and presence. There aren't too many of those out there.

And besides, her husband Greg is a restaurant-owner and fantastic cook.

Carla and Greg Overbeck

171

Cindy Parlow: CP (for Cindy Parlow if you haven't figured that out yet) has been fun to watch. She's a tall player, around 5-10 or 5-11, and pigeon toed. I love that. For one reason, I am also tall and pigeon toed, but the second reason is she makes for an imposing figure and easy target, as in someone to bang the ball into as she posts up or checks back, not someone we constantly shoot at or make fun of. Her stature makes her easy to find on the field.

CP came in as a quiet college player, a youngster, and has shown great promise. I know she is tearing it up at the college level, and I am sure she will be around the National Team for a while. And lastly, there is one thing I cannot leave out. Remember the Lobster feast? Well, CP was the master chef behind the mashed potatoes. Mmm. Mmm. Good.

Tiffany Roberts

Tiffany Roberts: TR. Another one of those initial-type nicknames. TR came in as a confident, indifferent youngster. Usually, when a young player comes in, they are a bit intimidated and stand off-ish. Not TR. She came right in and started banging heads. She is also one of those teen-idol kind of kids. She always has the hip, in-style clothes and listens to that new-wave-whatever kind of music. I feel like a parent when I am around her (I never quite understand what's going on with those kids now a days.) She's also a big shopper. Brandi and I always have her come into the room to model her latest shopping spree so we can keep up with the hip stuff and make fun of her outfit choices.

Besides being Miss Teen Idol, TR is a great athlete. Fit as anything. We wear heart-rate monitors at times to measure the intensity of the workout and the reaction of the body. TR's heart rate sometimes gets up to 100. That's inhuman. For most people they are either having a heart attack at that point, or gasping for breath with their hands on the knees. Only the elite of the elite athletes get up to 100 without dying. Well, for her, that's a normal occurrence. She can hit it, maintain it for a few seconds, and then keep on performing with little or no recovery time needed. Amazing. Oh to be young again.

Briana Scurry: Pronounced Br-eye-anna. Everyone gets it wrong, including me, and I want to set the record straight for her. The answer to the next question is, yes, she did run naked through the streets of Athens after we won the Gold. It's on video tape (yikes!), but I think by now, it has either been locked in a vault or burned up.

Bri is a great keeper. And I don't throw around the word "great" loosely. She is great! World-class great. I often tell people she plays like a man. That's the ultimate compliment in my book. I go out to keeper practice almost every session and have had the luxury of whacking about a million shots at her. You know the shots when you know it's going in, so you kind of turn around and jog back for the next ball before it actually goes in? Well, I have learned I can't do that with Bri. She gets to those. I have to watch them go in. I have to put that ball in the absolute corner or else Bri saves it. She is great, and I'm glad she's on our team.

Briana Scurry

Steve Slain: Steve-o. He is a literal God-send. As I said before, I met Steve due to injury, and we have been fast friends ever since. I think he's the greatest. We have a long history of butting heads, battling, training, hanging out, going to church together, and now with the National Team. Not only have I benefited from his massage-man hands and strength-training expertise, but his support and inspiration as a person have made a difference in my life. I know the team would agree. On top of all that great stuff, Christ has a tight hold on him, and I foresee him making a huge difference in this world through his special talents and commitment as a Christian. You rule, Steve.

Thori Staples: Thorni is a good friend. I love Thorni, in fact. She gave me one of my favorite verses from the Bible (Philippians 3:14 "I press on toward the goal to win the prize in which God has called me upward in Christ Jesus") and she is just one of those people with a truly tender heart.

Thorni was on the bubble for a long period and fought and fought and fought to be on this team. It hasn't been easy for her. She is a track athlete by trade — fast as all get out. So she had to learn

Thori and her mom

to adjust her training and focus to the different demands of soccer. It's been tough, but, she has never given up. I admire that about her. She doesn't have the most skillful game and is a little raw, but with Thorni you always get one-hundred percent effort. She will bust a gut for you. I would choose her for my team any day of the week.

One story about Thorni: Her little cousin (phonetically, her name is Ieesha) is a big fan of ours, and Thorni's parents always travel to the matches and bring her cute, little cousin. Well, before one game, Thorn told me what she got Ieesha for her birthday (a barbie or something). And me, thinking the birthday had already passed, saw her after the game and said, "So, Happy Birthday! Did you like the barbie Thorni got you?" Well, Thorni and her Mom just about ripped my head off. Jeez, I felt like a jerk. Another Akers mess up! Par for the course.

Tisha Venturini: Vench. Tish is someone I haven't gotten to know very well yet. But I have the utmost respect and admiration for her as a player, and from the little time we have spent together, I think she's cool. She has that "cool" quality for which not many people can qualify. It's more than being nice, or stylish, or charismatic. She's just cool and unique. I also know my brother's friends think she's "hot." That cracks me up. Not because I think she is a dog by any means, but because the public sees my teammates — my buddies — as hot. Ha.

Anyway, the reason why Tish and I haven't hung out is because we are both kind of shy, I think. We are close in a roundabout kind of way ... in fact, she was one of those who left me a note when I got whacked in the '95 World Cup. I like Tish. She is a brilliant midfielder, a great header, and I'm sure she'll be an integral part of this team for a long time to come.

Staci Wilson: Staci is an up-and-coming player. She was going through some stuff in '96, but she managed to hang tough and battle her way on to the Olympic Team. A trademark of Staci as a player is her incredible ferocity. She is scary in a good kind of way. She will not hesitate a moment to cut you in half for the ball ... which is deceiving when you first match up against her. She is this short, muscular little girl and you think she can't hit that hard. But she does. She is fearless. And she can jump! Here I'm 5-10, and she is out jumping me!

Me: Just a last little note. Now that I have totally disclosed all my teammates nicknames, I think it only fair to give you a few of mine. These names are either made up by my loving teammates or were heard from some announcer that totally butchered my name and now provides laughs for years and years to come. Ha. Ha. Very funny. Anyway, here's a few of them.

Akes. Mich (as in Mish). Mufasa. Mooof. Mich-Mich. Meeeesh. Big Hair. Lion Head. Geeeg. (G.G. for Glamour Girl courtesy of Foudy). Anchor-steem (from Akers-

Stahl). Aerosal or Arkansas (another Akers-Stahl aberration). Epstein. And lastly, Grace (because of my incredible coordination — not). Well, that's just a few off the top of my head to, hopefully, take the edge off the hot water I've gotten myself into with my teammates. I hope it was insightful and entertaining.

I did this book to tell you about my life and career, but also to share my team with you. They are cool people. Special people. And they deserve to be portrayed as heroes and role models. I hope you have seen how we are much more than just a bunch of soccer players. It is important to us that you know there are people behind the Gold Medals and World Cup trophies and our commitment is not only to be our best on the field, but to give and be our best for each other. That's an important distinction. I encourage and challenge you to do the same.

Now, on to the future. Everyone asks me, what's next? Well, I want to take this opportunity to share my new hopes and dreams and plans for the future. I have chosen to play in the 1999 World Cup and 2000 Olympics. Then I will retire. In the meantime, however, I am training/rehabbing for those two events and preparing for after.

What's after? Currently, I am going to seminary school (a school to learn about God) and plan to get my first degree in biblical theology (by 2000) and also hope to build a sports ministry through my church. What is sports ministry? Well, it is like this: I figure the church focuses on almost every part of your life except your physical body. What's up with that? I mean, why can't sports be a part of the church? Athletes are Christians too, and I would like to see people like me encouraged to play sports or keep fit and grow as a Christian through that experience. I think athletics and physical training can teach us a lot about what it's like to be a Christian and how God wants us to live our lives. Think about it — commitment, discipline, focus, sacrifice, winning and losing, hardship and pain, and team, just to name a few. I even read in a bible commentary that says "Christians are the athletes of Christ." Why can't the church be the governing body which facilitates, trains, and prepares its athletes to do God's work? Needless to say, I am ready to rock and roll in sports ministry. What could be more exciting?

Appendix B

Chronic Fatigue Immune Dysfunction Syndrome

IN 1984 AND '85, A LARGE NUMBER OF PEOPLE LIVING IN INCLINE VILLAGE, Nevada, were devastated by a mysterious and debilitating disease, now known to be Chronic Fatigue Immune Dysfunction Syndrome. Around the same time, University of California medical school professor Carol Jessop began seeing women patients who presented a baffling array of symptoms — fever, lymphadenopathy, sore throat, visual and other neurological disturbances, and paralytic muscle weakness. These symptoms got worse with minor physical exertion, forming a common denominator in all the cases. But when Jessop began subjecting the patients to exhaustive tests to rule out auto-immune and other diseases, male colleagues scoffed, calling the tests "million dollar workups on neurotic women."

After a quick and somewhat incomplete investigation of the outbreak in Incline Village, the Centers for Disease Control (CDC) and the National Institute of Health made little effort to aggressively research the illness. The problem of public perception was worsened by the 1988 Centers for Disease Control case definition that labeled the crippling disease with the word "fatigue."

"Chronic Fatigue Syndrome is a name that reveals just how tenuous the connection between words and their referents can be," wrote sufferer Maryann Spurgin in an article called 'Chronic Obfuscation.' "It is difficult to imagine clinical severity after hearing a name that denotes tiredness." In addition, government CFIDS investigators were continually suggesting the disease was a psychiatric problem, not a physical one, and they routinely discounted research that indicated otherwise. The message was that CFIDS sufferers should "get out and get their muscles working, get some exercise," when in fact this was exactly the wrong approach.

Two doctors — Paul Cheney and Dan Peterson — had a clinic in Incline Village to explore the illness, and they were the first to actively recognize and fight for the illness. They continuously badgered the CDC to come back to Nevada when they felt the initial investigation was inadequate. Cheney and Peterson enlisted experts in the medical community to begin researching the cause, effects and reality of CFIDS. It was not until 1995 — ten years after the Incline Village outbreak — that scientists at the CDC gave CFIDS a "Priority 1" listing among their "New and Reemerging Infectious Diseases" category. However, this did little to help Michelle. Because of the lack of understanding of CFIDS and its victims, Michelle's insurance still does not cover much of her treatment, tests and hospital bills — CFIDS is not a "recognized illness," they say.

A Harvard Research Team determined that approximately two million Americans suffer from Chronic Fatigue Immune Dysfunction Syndrome, four times as many as have Multiple Sclerosis. In addition, the Harvard group suggested the illness has an attack rate of 300 for every 100,000 Americans, a phenomenal number for such a debilitating illness. During the height of the polio epidemic in 1953, for example, the attack rate of paralytic polio was 20 per 100,000 Americans. While the attack rate is thought to be high, the rate of recovery, it seems, is low. Studies have shown that full recovery is a rare event — somewhere in the four- to eight-percent range. And after five years with the illness, chances for full recovery are even lower. Many, if not most, CFIDS patients do improve over time — although "time" in this case means years. A portion of CFIDS sufferers never improve, and some deteriorate. Treatments are available, but as Michelle discovered, most seem to be of little help. However, everyone responds differently, and in some instances, sufferers have shown significant improvement.

Included in what is still unknown about CFIDS are its causes and origin. Some cases of people with similar symptoms were documented in the 1930s, 40s and 50s. That older disease was called Epidemic Neuromyastherua. But the cause of the illness remains unknown today. Current theories are looking at the possibilities of neuroendocrine dysfunction, viruses, environmental toxins, genetic predisposition, or a combination of these. For a time, it was thought the Epstein-Barr Virus — the cause of mononucleosis — might cause CFIDS, but recent research discounts the notion. Chronic Fatigue Immune Dysfunction Syndrome seems to prompt a chronic immune reaction in the body. However, it is not clear whether the reaction is in response to any actual infection. It may be only a malfunction of the immune system itself. A recently introduced theory is that CFIDS is a generalized condition which may have any of several causes — in the same way that high blood pressure is not caused by any one single factor. It is known, however, that emotional or physical stress seems to make CFIDS worse. Many medical observers have noted that CFIDS often seems to be triggered by some stressful event, and it's likely the condition was dormant before the stressful event. Some people will appear to get CFIDS following a viral infection, a head injury, surgery, excessive use of antibiotics, or some other traumatic event. Yet it's unlikely that these events — on their own — could be the primary cause.

177

What is CFIDS?

CFIDS (chronic fatigue and immune dysfunction syndrome) is also known as CFS (chronic fatigue syndrome), CEBV (chronic Epstein Barr virus), M.E. (myalgic encephalomyelitis), "yuppie flu" and many other names. It is a complex illness characterized by incapacitating fatigue (experienced as exhaustion and extremely poor stamina), neurological problems and a constellation of symptoms that can resemble other disorders, including: mononucleosis, multiple sclerosis, fibromyalgia, AIDS-related complex (ARC), Lyme disease, post-polio syndrome and auto-immune diseases such as lupus. These symptoms tend to wax and wane but are often severely debilitating and may last for many months or years. All segments of the population (including children) are at risk, but women under the age of forty-five seem to be the most susceptible.

What causes CFIDS?

Research suggests that CFIDS results from a dysfunction of the immune system. The exact nature of this dysfunction is not yet well-defined, but it can generally be viewed as an up-regulated or overactive state (which is responsible for many of the symptoms). Ironically, there is also evidence of some immune suppression in CFIDS; patients exhibit certain down-regulated signs.

For example, in many patients there are functional deficiencies in natural killer cells (an important component of the immune system responsible for protection against viruses). Based on physical and laboratory findings, many scientists are convinced that viruses are associated with CFIDS and may be directly involved in causing the disease.

Since the discovery (or rediscovery) of CFIDS in the United States in the mid-1980s, several viruses have been and continue to be studied to determine what, if any, part they play in the disease. These include enteroviruses, herpesviruses (especially human herpesvirus-6 or HHV-6) and newly discovered retroviruses.

In the first few years of this research, it was thought that the Epstein-Barr virus (EBV), a herpesvirus that causes mononucleosis, was the cause of this syndrome. However, researchers now believe that EBV activation (when it exists) is a result or complication of CFIDS rather than its cause. To date, no virus has been conclusively shown to be an essential element of CFIDS. Accordingly, research efforts are still directed toward identifying and isolating the fundamental agent(s) responsible for triggering immune system disruption in persons with CFIDS (PWCs).

Additionally, there are on-going studies of immunologic, neurologic and metabolic abnormalities and co-factors (such as genetic predisposition, age, sex, prior illness, other viruses, environment and stress) which appear to play an important role in the development and course of the illness.

For further information see The CFIDS Chronicle which reports extensively on all aspects of CFIDS research and/or call The CFIDS Information Line (900/896-2343) for the most recent developments in CFIDS research.

How is CFIDS Diagnosed?

Many physicians base their diagnosis of CFIDS on a "working case definition" developed by the Centers for Disease Control (CDC) and published in the March 1988 Annals of Internal Medicine. To meet the CDC case definition, a patient must fulfill two "major criteria" and either eight of eleven "symptom criteria" or six of the symptom criteria and two of three "physical criteria."

The major criteria are:

1. "New onset of persistent or relapsing, debilitating fatigue or easy fatigability in a person who has no previous history of similar symptoms, that does not resolve with bedrest and that is severe enough to reduce or impair average daily activity below fifty percent of the patient's premorbid activity level for a period of at least six months."

2. Exclusion of other plausible disorders "by thorough evaluation, based on history, physical examination and appropriate laboratory findings."

The CDC's symptom criteria include onset of the symptom complex over a few hours or days. The CDC's physical criteria, which must be documented on at least two occasions, at least one month apart, are: low-grade fever, nonexudative pharyngitis (sore throat) and palpable or tender lymph nodes. The CDC has stated that this definition is only "an operational concept" and that it may therefore fail to include many persons who have this syndrome.

Although the CDC case definition is in some sense "official" (and legitimizes the illness), it is considered provisional because it is based on symptoms which can be produced by other diseases and on the exclusion of such diseases. Fortunately, pioneering CFIDS clinicians and researchers are making great strides in identifying specific objective markers for diagnosing CFIDS and for assessing patient treatment response. As reported in The CFIDS Chronicle (see especially, "CFIDS: The Diagnosis Of A Distinct Illness," September 1992), physicians and scientists in California, Canada, Florida, North Carolina, Texas, Wisconsin and elsewhere are developing an array of tests which are increasingly sensitive and specific for CFIDS. As the cause and mechanism of this disease become clear so will the clinical and laboratory parameters which define CFIDS. Ultimately, conclusive diagnostic standards will be developed and accepted.

Unfortunately, many physicians are not very familiar with CFIDS and have difficulty diagnosing it. Others still do not even know that the illness exists. As a result, PWCs (Persons With CFIDS) are often misdiagnosed, sometimes as having a psychosomatic or affective disorder because such conditions are also diagnosed by exclusion in many cases. What are the symptoms? PWCs experience symptoms which tend to be individualistic and to fluctuate in severity. According to the CDC case definition, symptoms may include: profound or prolonged fatigue, especially after exercise levels that would have been easily tolerated before; low grade fever; sore throat; painful lymph nodes; muscle weakness; muscle discomfort or myalgia (pain or aching); sleep disturbance (hypersomnia or insomnia); headaches of a new type, severity, or pattern; migratory arthralgia without joint swelling or redness; neuropsychologic problems including photophobia, transient visual scotomata (spots), forgetfulness, irritability, confusion, difficulty thinking, inability to concentrate and depression. Further symptoms common to CFIDS could include other cognitive function problems (such as spatial disorientation and dyslogia — impairment of speech and or reasoning), visual disturbances (blurring, sensitivity to light, eye pain, frequent prescription changes) and psychological problems (anxiety, panic attacks, personality changes, emotional instability); chills and night sweats; shortness of breath; dizziness and balance problems; sensitivity to heat and cold; intolerance of alcohol; irregular heartbeat; abdominal pain, diarrhea, irritable bowel; low temperature; numbness of or burning in the face or extremities; dryness of the mouth and eyes (sicca syndrome); hearing disorders or sensitivity; menstrual problems including PMS and endometriosis; hypersensitivity of the skin; chest pains; rashes; allergies and sensitivities to odors, chemicals and medications; weight changes without changes in diet; hair loss; lightheadedness (feeling "in a fog"); fainting; muscle twitching; and seizures.

How Can CFIDS be Treated and What is the Prognosis?

No primary therapy has been proven to cure CFIDS. However, experimental treatments are being evaluated in clinical trials. In addition, some symptoms frequently can be alleviated by prescription drugs (such as Klonopin, Prozac, Sinequan, Xanax and Zantac), but these must be carefully tailored to the needs of each individual and often must be taken in unusually low dosages. Also, avoidance of environmental irritants and certain foods can sometimes relieve symptoms and many PWCs claim to have benefited from nutritional therapies. A significant percentage of PWCs show marked improvement over time. But many remain ill or cycle through a continuing series of remissions and relapses. The symptoms in severely-affected PWCs can be devastating and result in prolonged interruption of work and family life. Some researchers believe that PWCs may also be at greater risk of developing other illnesses. However, the extent to which CFIDS may be progressive or degenerative is not yet known. For additional information on treatment options and prognosis see The CFIDS Chronicle or call The CFIDS Information Line.

Is CFIDS Contagious?

It is probable that the viruses and/or other agents that trigger CFIDS are transmissible. CFIDS has been reported in many children and monogamous adults and "clustering" of cases in families, workplaces and communities also seems to occur. Anecdotal reports exist of pets of CFIDS patients getting unusual diseases. However, whether a person develops CFIDS is believed to be a function of how his or her system deals with the causative agent(s). Most people in close contact with CFIDS patients have not developed the illness.

How Does One Live With CFIDS?

Persons with CFIDS must identify their limits and learn to operate within them. Symptoms tend to be aggravated by physical or emotional stress and improved by rest. Those who accept the fact that they have a chronic illness and regulate their lives accordingly generally cope better than those who deny the reality of their illness. Many PWCs overcome the sense of isolation and helplessness common to the disease by joining support groups and working to help each other. In telephone calls, newsletters, journals and at meetings and conferences they share experiences, exchange information and learn from each other. PWCs often find an equilibrium point at which they can function. As in combating any chronic illness, a positive, hopeful attitude is essential.

Which Physicians Understand CFIDS?

Finding a physician knowledgeable about CFIDS can be difficult. The symptoms are not organ-specific and no single medical discipline has embraced the disease. Individuals who have been diagnosed with CFIDS are excellent sources of referrals and a Physicians Honor Roll of CFIDS clinicians (nominated by their patients) is available from The CFIDS Association of America, Inc.

In addition, a list of physicians knowledgeable about CFIDS is maintained by most local support groups. However, if you already have a good relationship with a doctor, you should urge him or her to develop an understanding of this disease — perhaps by sending him or her several issues of The CFIDS Chronicle.

181

What Can Be Done To Help?

This has been and continues to be a movement driven by PWCs seeking to help themselves. Please join us and the many thousands striving to overcome CFIDS. Fight back! Contribute! Volunteer! Attend or establish a local support group. Write to members of Congress or the media. Become a member of The CFIDS Association of America, Inc. Our objectives are to encourage and inform PWCs, their physicians, families and friends and to fund increased research into the mechanism and treatment of CFIDS. We are a non-profit organization governed by an all-volunteer board of directors comprised of PWCs and professionals. We publish the largest CFIDS journal in the nation, The CFIDS Chronicle, and directly fund CFIDS research and CFIDS advocacy efforts. All funds contributed to The CFIDS Association of America, Inc. for a specific valid CFIDS purpose are so allocated one-hundred percent!

In accordance with this, a special fund has also been set up called The Michelle Akers CFIDS Fund (through the CFIDS Association of America) to support youth and athletes with CFIDS, as well as, friends, family, and those who know people with CFIDS. It is our goal to educate and support those who are sick and encourage the government, media, medical community and public to help influence and promote the research of and treatment for CFIDS.

For more information, please call 800-442-3437.

The Michelle Akers CFIDS Fund

This fund is to support youths and athletes with CFIDS, as well as friends, family and those who know people with CFIDS. The CFIDS Association of America and I wish to educate and support those who are sick and encourage the media, government, medical community and the general public to help influence and promote research of and treatment for CFIDS. For more information or to contribute, call 1-800-442-3437.

Produced and distributed by The CFIDS Association of America, Inc., PO Box 220398, Charlotte, North Carolina 28222-0398, 800/442-3437, The CFIDS Information Line 900/896-2343, FAX 704/365-9755. Edited by Paul R. Cheney, MD, Ph.D., Charles W. Lapp, MD and David S. Bell, MD, medical consultants to The CFIDS Association of America, Inc. Some of the information contained herein is intended to help PWCs make informed decisions about their health. For medical advice, please consult with your physician.

Appendix C

CFIDS Information Sources Support Organizations

CFIDS Association of America
P O Box 220398
Charlotte, NC 28222-0398
Answering machine: 800-442-3437 (44-CFIDS) or 1-704-362-2343
Information line: 900-988-2343 (988-CFID) $2.00 1st minute, $1.00 ea. thereafter
Fax line: 1-704-365-9755
Membership: $25/yr, includes subscription to "CFIDS Chronicle"
Magazine services: Will provide list of local support contacts, also list of physicians recommended by local patients; they raise funds for medical research; lobby U.S. Congress to influence health policy; the Chronicle magazine is excellent.

Dr Peter Rowe
Tilt Table Diagnostic Laboratory
Johns Hopkins Medical Institution
600 North Wolfe St/Brady 604
Baltimore, MD 21287
Ph. 410-614-4823 or 800-624-4562 • Fx. 410-614-9308
Note: Contact Dr. Rowe for information on treatment and diagnosis of Neurally Mediated Hypotension

National CFS and Fibromyalgia Association
3521 Broadway / Suite 222
Kansas City, MO 64111
Telephone: 1-816-931-4777
Available: Quarterly newsletter $15/yr.; general information packet $1; patient info. packet $15; physician's packet $10; how to be a phone contact $4; how to form a support group $6; CFS info. bibliography $3.50.
Note: Newsletter is excellent, oriented to scientifically validated information on CFS and FMS
CFIDS Treatment News (about twice yearly) from CFIDS Foundation, 965 Mission St., Suite 425, San Francisco, CA 94103, USA.
Subscription in exchange for donation of any amount (tax exempt).

The Update (quarterly) — from the Mass. CFIDS Assoc., 808 Main St., Waltham, MA 02154, USA. $15.00 per year.

Canada
The Nightingale Foundation
383 Danforth Avenue
Ottawa, Ontario K2A 0E1
Telephone: 1-613-728-9643
Membership: $35/yr. includes quarterly newsletter
Services: they support a network of local support groups; publish a CFS medical encyclopedia edited by Dr. Byron White, MD

M.E. Association
246 Queen Street Suite 400
Ottawa, Ontario K1P 5E4
Telephone: 1-613-563-1565
Membership: $35/yr. includes monthly newsletter "The MEssenger"; list of medical articles regarding CFS/ME provided on request.

United Kingdom
M.E. Action
P.O Box 1302
Wells, Somerset BA5 2WE
United Kingdom
Membership: About #14/yr. includes Interaction journal 3 times/yr.
Activities: Works in partnership with over 200 local M.E. support groups, many of whom actively raise public awareness of the illness through media and local MPs etc.
Publications:
• Interaction journal w/o membership is #5 per year; available on tape #2 per issue, cheque payable to ME Tapes, send to Melanie Kelly, 29 Blandfield Road, London, SW12 8BQ
• Therapy Information Pack, 9 factsheets on a comprehensive range of M.E therapies (Members #2:50, Non-Members #3:50)
• Supplementary Factsheets 35p each: Information for Doctors, to help your GP
• A Guide for the Non-sufferer, to educate friends, relatives and work colleagues. Information for Employers
• Advice for Young Sufferers, i.e. under 25

Electronic Information Sources

• For information of CFIDS, see Michelle's homepage — www.michelleakers.com

• The CFS mailing list/ alt.med.cfs: Those who are looking a patients' discussion of health and other issues should join the CFS-L list based at LISTSERV@LIST.NIH.GOV (or on BITNET at LISTSERV@NIHLIST);The CFS mailing list is identical to the Usenet newsgroup alt.med.cfs.

• CFS file archives: It is possible to transfer many informational text files on CFS over the Internet by e-mail. There are current two main Internet CFS file archives. The Albany Listserv is at address LISTSERV@ALBNYDH2.BITNET or alternatively LIST-SERV%ALBNYDH2.BITNET@ALBANY.EDU. To get a list of available files, send the message GET CFS-D FILELIST to the above address. To get any specific file, send the message GET filename1 filename2 (each file has a two-part name). For example, to retrieve the latest version of the CFS Electronic Resources Guide, by Roger Burns (which is named CFS-RES TXT), send the message GET CFS-RES TXT. To automatically receive future notices about updates to the CFS filelist, create the message SUD CFS D your name where your name replaces your name, and send it to the LISTSERV address shown above.

A new base of CFS information files is being developed at the SJUVM Listserv. To get a listing of available files, send the message GET CFS-FILE FILELIST to the address LISTSERV@SJUVM.STJOHNS.EDU or to LISTSERV@SJUVM.BITNET. To get any specific file, send the message GET filename1 filename2 (each file has a two-part name) to the Listserv address above.

• CFS Electronic Newsletter: Current medical research updates can be obtained by subscribing to CFS-NEWS, the Chronic Fatigue Syndrome Electronic Newsletter. The newsletter is posted to the CFS "echo" (or conference) on Fidonet (see the next item). On the Internet, e-mail subscriptions are available from LISTSERV at NIHLIST.BIT-NET or LIST.NIH.GOV, or simply send an e-mail inquiry to the address CFS-NEWS@LIST.NIH.GOV

Appendix D

Choosing To Live

WHEN YOU ARE FACING A CHRONIC ILLNESS, EVENTUALLY YOU are forced to accept the fact that your life will never be the same — *you* will never be the same. Or in the very least, you won't be able to hang on to the same activities and responsibilities you had before, because the illness limits you so severely physically, and sometimes, even mentally. There is tremendous grief because in a sense a part of you is dying. What you thought you were is stripped away and what you are left with is something, someone you don't recognize, don't want, or don't even like. Some get mad, others sad, some feel frustration, and still others lash out or withdraw into themselves in reaction to the ravages of CFIDS. And then, eventually, you somehow accept it. Not give up or give in, but accept it. You accept the circumstances and the limits the illness imposes on you. You learn to rest, to have peace and still be sick. You never stop fighting and striving for recovery, but learn not to react or run from the pain. You even learn to turn into it. You choose how you respond, choose the attitude you will take. You realize you are not a victim. You choose to live.

Now, to be clear, accepting the illness and accepting oneself are two very different things. Yes, I finally found the courage to accept CFIDS and even look at who I had become, but that was far from accepting or loving this new person I had become — limitations and all. My saving grace was having God in my life. It took knowing God to find the courage to accept myself no matter what condition I was in. God ultimately gave me the key to accept myself as is — with CFIDS, and maybe without soccer. Sick or healthy. That is the key to facing and accepting oneself and to finally, overcoming.

I WENT PUBLIC WITH MY ILLNESS IN THE HOPES THAT PEOPLE COULD benefit from my struggle. At first, of course, I was reluctant to allow people into the private hell that had exploded inside me. It was just too overwhelming, too revealing, too painful and too risky. But then I realized I was in a unique position. My platform as a world-class athlete allowed me the opportunity to contribute in a very powerful way to the fight and plight of people stricken by CFIDS. I could be the voice for those who could not speak for themselves. I could change the face of CFIDS, not only for myself, but for the world. I could make a difference.

I soon learned, however, that a part of the CFIDS community was upset with me, because in short, I was not acting sick enough. It seems the CFIDS population is split on me going public and becoming a spokesperson of sorts for CFIDS sufferers. The feeling, as I understand it, is that I am demeaning the tragedy and the severity of the illness by playing soccer, by fighting for my life, by not giving in. They think I cannot possibly have CFIDS and be an Olympic athlete.

How did I do it? Or maybe more importantly, how do I keep on doing it? What do I have that makes me different from them? I am a professional, world-class athlete. I was one of the best players in the world. Before I got sick, it was my daily routine to train four-to-six hours a day at the highest level of physical fitness. I have trained my entire life to push up to and beyond the limits of my physical capacities. I am experienced at being physically uncomfortable or feeling the "burn" of a tough workout. For an athlete, pain is an indicator of a good workout. It's an obstacle to overcome as you compete for a trophy. Pain is something you put on the shelf to feel at a later time. I have played with many injuries and found that most of the pain is in my head. I can control it to some extent and learn to live with it. I am an expert at hearing and feeling the signals of when my body has had enough ... and then pushing on further. That's what a world-class athlete does. That is how we become the best.

When I became sick, however, I found that even this will, this world-class determination and focus, was not enough to sustain me. At my sickest, I couldn't ride a stationary bike for more than five minutes without collapse. My physical capacities were severely diminished. My mental strength was not enough. It was all I could do to hang on. In fact, if I had been a "normal" person, I would have given up long ago. So you see, I was very sick. In fact, sick enough to be deemed worthy of citizenship in the CFIDS community. However, what the world saw on the soccer field was my best face. They saw my best effort, my only reserve, and the discipline of many years of hiding and shelving the pain of exhaustion and weariness. What they did not see was the utter decimation that inevitably followed.

Unfortunately, this is a common struggle for lots of people with CFIDS. We all fall into a lose-lose scenario. If you are really sick — totally disabled — you don't fit into the real world, and you feel lost, isolated. But even worse, if you are sick but able to function, albeit in a diminished capacity, you don't fit in with either world — the sick or the healthy. CFIDS people don't accept you and the healthy world can't relate. You can't win. It is my desire to change that. So, now I am realizing there is more to being sick than being sick. The repercussions of chronic illness are endless and all-encompassing. My initial ambition in going public was to help CFIDS sufferers overcome the illness, but now I am understanding the battles we face with CFIDS are just an extreme side of the battles faced by all of us. At one time or another, we all face anguish, loss, confusion, and fear. We all lose our identity, or we find the resources we once relied so heavily upon are not enough. We all face disappointment, anger, and frustration.

CFIDS has forced me to make my battles, inadequacies and triumphs public. I cannot stand by and see countless suffer and plod through life without hope when I could have encouraged them with my unique and yet, prevalent experiences. Although, I resisted at first, CFIDS has become an open door to tell the world about the hope I have found. It's a hope that can never be crushed, or diminished, or dulled. CFIDS has become an avenue to tell the world about the incredible grace and strength of God and what He can do if we just let Him. My life is a witness to His power, His love, His mercy and His Strength. People wonder how I have managed to play soccer, to be a gold medalist, and be sick with CFIDS. Yes, it has to do with my training, and my stubborn, persistent personality. It also had to do with the unique physical condition I was in when I developed the illness. But mostly it has to do with God's hold on my life. He has refused to drop me. He is the one holding me up and carrying me onward.

And the fight has been worth it. Recently, I received a promising prognosis from a chronic illness specialist. In February, I was told I may be able to fully recover and be one-hundred percent healthy in as short a time as four months. For the first time in my life, I have the chance to be totally and completely healthy and have the correct focus and priorities in my life. And you know what? I am eternally grateful for the illness. Sure, I can say, that now ... I'm out of the woods. But, what you forget is I have been saying that same thing in even my darkest moments. If it wasn't for the darkness, I would never have been able to see the stars.

The fight is worth it. Don't give up. Keep striving. You will not be disappointed. Your day of rejoicing will come and you will finally know you are stronger and more powerful than you ever dreamed.

Appendix E
A Message From Michelle

Hey there!

I am so glad you turned to this page! It has been our hope that my story would not only encourage, enlighten, and inspire you to persevere despite long odds or tough times, but also intrigue you enough to take one step closer to knowing God.

The most wonderful thing I have learned since I gave my life to Christ is that this Christian stuff not only creates and inspires a power within and a passion for life, but this Christian stuff is also personal, alive and real.

I was just about knocked off my rocker when I first realized something so completely opposite from my past impressions of God and his followers. You see, I thought of God in relation to the churches I had attended as a kid — hard, wooden benches, stiff and boring preachers, and judgmental, prim and proper, lifeless followers — certainly not a God or a group of people that I could relate to, live up to, or even want to be around. No joy, no hope, no fun! I thought if that was the kind of God they followed and that was how Christians were supposed to act, I could do much better on my own.

Unfortunately, I still come across those stiff and joyless church-goers of my childhood. But the sad thing for them and the good news for us is they have totally missed the point! Being a Christian is not about rules, or acting a certain way, reciting Bible verses, or knowing all the hymns at Sunday service. Being a Christian is about knowing a living and breathing God. Being a Christian means throwing your head back, charging through, over, and around the impossibilities of life and living each day to its fullest in the knowledge and confidence that God is with you.

This truth is important for me to convey because it is something I missed for many years. I think it took me so long to understand because, in short, I thought I knew everything. I thought I had all the answers. I thought I had the strength, and the means to know joy, happiness and success in life. Boy was I wrong! When all resources failed, and I stood alone looking for something to bail me out, I was forced to acknowledge the fact that there is something more to this life than me and my now-inadequate resources.

When I really started to look at the scheme of life closely, I thought, "I can't just be here to win soccer trophies and championships." I mean, when it's all said and done, who really cares if you're the best in the world or you make the most money or have the hippest clothes, or if you are fat or skinny or bald or whatever? I knew I was missing something.

That is the moment, I said okay to God. "Here is your shot," I told him. "I am giving you my wrecked body and life. Let's see what you can do with it." Well, to my surprise, God started to clean house. It took the better part of a year, searching and striving to know and understand Him just a little. But eventually, I found that giving your life to God has nothing to do with the stiffness, the judgment, the rigidity of the church I had known before. And it has everything to do with joy, love, grace, forgiveness and power. I was so psyched!

People that truly know and love God are those that shine. They aren't the ones who look down their noses at you. They are the ones that love you without limits. They are selfless. They give! They serve. And they are full of a joy that's just not normal. They have a confidence and a wisdom that surpass anyone you have ever met. They are different. They are the people that make you wonder what it is they know or have that you don't. Have you figured it out yet? I finally did. It's God. God is the difference in their lives, and now I have him too.

The cool thing is God wants you to know him too. And he waits ever so patiently for you to turn to him. Christ is available to everyone, no matter who you are, no matter what you have done, or what you're facing. He will change your life. And you know what? It's free. That's why they call it the "gift of grace." We can't earn it and we certainly don't deserve it. God loves each of us so much that He let His Son die, so we could know Him personally. God only asks you to make yourself available to Him, that you choose Him. Then, look out! You are in for the ride of your life.

So whether you accept Christ now, tomorrow, or years from now, I am glad I got to share what God has done with me and for me. He is amazing and full of surprises. I often wonder why it took me so long to just let him take the driver's seat. There is no greater, more challenging, or more fulfilling ride than the one God has set before me. There is certainly no one else I want waiting for me as my ride comes to its final turn. Who will be there for you?

In God's grace and power,
Michelle

Four Principles of Faith

If you are interested in knowing God through Christ Jesus, here are some principles that will help guide you in your first steps toward a new life in Christ.

One Love. One Purpose.

Know that God loves you and he created you to know him personally.

Get that through your head first. You know how your dad, or mom, family, or best friend loves you? Well, triple that love a hundred thousand million infinite times and that's how much God loves you. The second thing to know is he created us to know him and have a relationship with him. It seems hard to believe that the God of the universe would want to relate to us, especially when we are such jerks or so dumb most of the time. But it's true. He really thinks we are something special.

He says it in the Bible lots of times, but here are a few examples:

• About God's love for us:

"God so loved the world, that he gave his only begotten son that whoever believes in him should not perish, but have eternal life" (John 3:16).

• About God's plan:

" ... I have come that they may have life, and have it to the fullest" (John 10:10).

God wants us to have it all! He allowed His Son to die for us, He loves us without limit, He has a specific plan for each of us, and our lives are meant be full, rich, and eternal. So, what is the hold up? Why doesn't everyone have this kind of life now? Sin. Sin is the hold up. Sin is the thing that gets between us and God and keeps us from experiencing all these wonderful things God has promised to us.

Now, before you get all riled up, and say "Well, I'm a good person. I am nice to my little brother and I take out the garbage for my Mom. I'm not a sinner!" The thing to remember is that God is *perfect*, and we are far, far from that. If you think about all the mean things we have done or mean thoughts that have crossed through our minds or negative emotions we have felt ... all those (even if we didn't *act* on them) are considered sinful in the eyes of God. It is important to understand the background and specific meaning of sin and how that plays into our experiencing the full grace and love of God.

We all fall way, way short.

We are separated from God because we are sinful, so we cannot know him personally or experience his love.

We were originally created to intimately know and hang out with God. But because we are so stubborn about doing things our way and want to follow our own desires, we choose ourselves over God. This choice is evident either outwardly and defiantly by words and or actions or by remaining indifferent or passive to God's call on our lives. This is what God calls sin. You see, when dealing with God, you are either in or you're out. There is no "kind of" or "a little bit" when dealing with God. It's all . . . or nothing. And when you don't follow him or give your life completely to him, you are separate and apart from his presence. We *all* fall into this category (so don't feel left out) until we make a change.

Here's what God says about it in the Bible:

• We are sinful and all fall short of God's holiness and perfection"

"All have sinned and fall short of the glory of God" (Romans 3:23).

• We are separated from God.

"The wages of sin is death" [spiritual separation from God] (Romans 6:23).

God is simply saying that he is perfect and blameless and we are not. When we choose ourselves over God, we are spiritually dead and lost. There is a huge chasm between God and his perfection and us and our imperfection. Picture yourself standing on one side of the Grand Canyon and God on the other. We cannot reach him through our efforts or by trying to be good, because nothing can bring us closer to God *except* God himself.

The Gift
Jesus Christ is God's only provision for our sin.

Because we can't cross the "Grand Canyon" of sin and imperfection on our own to meet him, God sent his son to be the bridge from him to us. A long time ago, God sent Jesus to die in our place so we can know him and hang out with him forever. Jesus Christ is God's son, and he came to earth to pay the penalty of wrongdoing in our stead.

It's as if each of us were sitting in a jail cell awaiting our day in the gas chamber to pay the cost of all the wrong (sin) we have done. Then God comes to each of our jail cells, and says, "Here. My Son will take your place. You are the one who deserves to die, as you are the one who has done wrong, but you have been pardoned. Why? Because I love you. I love you so much, I am sending my son who has done nothing and is blameless and perfect, and He will take your place." And then, Jesus willingly dies for you. Jesus is killed. And you are free. Pretty awesome when you think about it. God, the perfect God, sends His only Son to die for us, so that we can know Him. And Christ willingly does it. He willingly tosses aside His power, riches, and glory in heaven to come to earth to be beaten, spit on, stabbed, humiliated, and eventually, nailed to a cross and killed all for the sake of God's immense love for us. All for the sake of ... you and me. His death is personal. His death is the only way for you and I to know God.

By God's design, you are able to know him only through Christ's paying the penalty (sacrifice) for you. There is only one way to know God and that is through his Son, Christ Jesus.

In the Bible it says this:

• Christ died in our place. "God demonstrated his own love toward us, in that while we are yet sinners, Christ died for us" (Romans 5:8).

• He rose from the dead. "Christ died for our sins ... he was buried ... he was raised on the third day, according to the Scriptures ... he appeared to Peter, then to the twelve. After that. he appeared to more than five hundred ..." (1 Corinthians 15:3-6).

• He is the only way to God. "Jesus said to him, "I am the way, the truth, and the life; no one comes to the father, but through me'" (John 14:6).

Okay, so Jesus died in our place, rose up, and appeared to the world alive and resurrected from death. It isn't enough just to know and believe that. You must do something. You must act. You must invite him to change your life and to live inside your heart.

By Invitation Only

We must individually receive Christ; then we can know God personally and experience His love.

We can only receive Christ through faith and by personal invitation. It takes faith to ask God into your heart and with this faith, you must ask Christ to be that bridge to God, to be your savior. You must personally choose Christ to be the foundation and center of your life. God will not force himself into our lives or choose for us. We must choose him.

God says the following about receiving Christ:

• It is through faith we must receive Him. "By grace you have been saved through faith; and that not of yourselves, it is gift of God; not as a result of works, that no one should boast" (Ephesians 2:8,9).

• [Christ says] "Behold, I stand at the door and knock; and if anyone hears my voice and opens the door, I will come in to him" (Revelation 3:20).

Christ knocks and knocks and knocks. He is tireless. But. he won't come in until you open the door. You have to do it. You must choose Him. He will never bust down the door. It's up to you to want to know Christ and when you decide, only then will he come in.

• When we receive Christ, we are born again: Read John 3:1-8.

193

A New Life.

It takes only a willing and sincere heart to ask God into your life.

To become a Christian, you need only say a short prayer (talk with God) to acknowledge the death of Christ in your place and your need for Christ to be at the center of your life. Don't worry about what you say to God. He is only concerned with your attitude and sincerity. Just talk from your heart.

If you can't find the words, let me help you. You can say this prayer. It is the same one I prayed to become a Christian when I was 14. Here goes:

> *Dear God, thanks so much for sending your son to die in my place. I want to know you personally. I want you to change my life. I want you to be the center of who I am. Thank you for forgiving my sins and giving me eternal life with you. Now, take my life and myself and make me who you want me to be, and give me the courage and strength to go where you want me to go. Amen.*

If you prayed this prayer with a sincere heart, Christ is now alive in you and is already beginning a new work in your life. Awesome! Now that you are a Christian and God is in your heart, here are some changes that have occurred whether you realize it yet or not:

1. Christ is in your life. (Rev. 3:20, Col. 1:27)
2. Your sins are forgiven. (Col. 1:14)
3. You are a child of God. (John 1:12)
4. You have eternal life. (John 5:24)
5. Buckle up! You are on the great adventure for which God created you. (John 10:10; 2 Cor. 5:17; I Thes. 5:18)

Now what?

The key now is to keep searching to know God by talking with him (prayer), reading about Him (in the Bible and other Christian books), going to church, and getting to know other Christians. The more you go to God daily in prayer, read the Bible, obey and trust God in even the tiny things, show and share your life in Christ with others, and allow the God to control and empower you, the more you will experience the incredible gifts and fullness of life with him. Your life will never be that same. Count on it.

Standing Fast

As a helpful reminder, don't rely on your feelings or emotions to see if God is within you. Much of the time, our feelings change and are unreliable. That's where faith comes in: God keeps his promises and he is there if you were sincere in your request to know him. You can trust him to keep his word.

As your faith grows and you get to know God better, you will start to understand his promises and even see them manifested in your life. Remember, He has a specific plan for your life and wants you to be joyful, loving, and fulfilled. Stand fast in the Lord and He will not let you down. You are His forever.

Free Stuff for Guidance

If you'd like more to information on knowing God and how to grow in your relationship with him, and this appendix and book have been helpful to you, please let us know. We not only want to hear your story, but want to send you some free stuff to help you grow as a Christian.

Send your letter to:
Integrated Resources
100 Sunport Lane
Orlando, FL 32809

(Principles paraphrased and adapted from a version of The Four Spiritual Laws by Bill Bright, Knowing God Personally, copyright 1965, 1988, Campus Crusade for Christ, Inc.)

Learn More About Michelle by reading her other book,

Face To Face with Michelle Akers

1-800-729-4351

● ● ● ● ● ● ●

You can also order

Ashes to Gold,

Michelle's audio tape of her testimony and life/soccer experiences

1-800-653-8333

● ● ● ● ● ● ●

Check out Michelle's internet homepage at

http://www.michelleakers.com

JTC Sports, Inc.

Standing Fast is the second book published by JTC Sports, Inc. during the company's three-year history. Founded in 1994 by Jan Cheves and Tim Nash, JTC Sports has been dedicated to providing innovative and original sports-related literature. "Training Soccer Champions", by Anson Dorrance and Tim Nash (published in 1996), has been widely recognized as a unique book about leadership, motivation and excellence. Other products by JTC Sports, Inc. include the highly respected monthly newspaper, Soccer News, the United States Women's National Soccer Team 1996 and 1997 Calendars, and the soon to be released children's book, The Sports Zoo.

To order **"Standing Fast"** or other

JTC Sports, Inc. products, call

1-800-551-9721

PO Box 513, Apex, NC 27502

Tim Nash

After completing **Standing Fast,** Tim Nash immediately began work on two more soccer book projects for JTC Sports, Inc., the company of which he is vice-president. **Standing Fast** is the second book co-authored by Nash. The first, Anson Dorrance's **Training Soccer Champions**, was published by JTC Sports in 1996.

The 38-year-old Nash has an extensive background in soccer, beginning at age four as a player. He played collegiately, and has coached soccer at the youth and high school levels.

Prior to starting JTC Sports, Inc. with his partner, Jan Cheves, Tim worked for seven years as a writer, editor and managing editor for collegiate and major league baseball team publications. He shifted his attention from college athletics and baseball to his first love, soccer, in 1993 with the creation of the national monthly publication, Soccer News. A year later, Tim and Jan purchased Soccer News and founded JTC Sports. He is now considered one of the top soccer writers in the country and an authority on American women's soccer.

A native of Oswego, N.Y., and a 10-year resident of Graham, N.C., Tim is married to the former Cheri Mitchum. They have one child, a five-year-old daughter, Allison.